Gaslighting

Learn How to Spot and Avoid the Gaslight Effect. Disarm the Narcissist and Heal from Emotional Abuse.

By Christina Covert

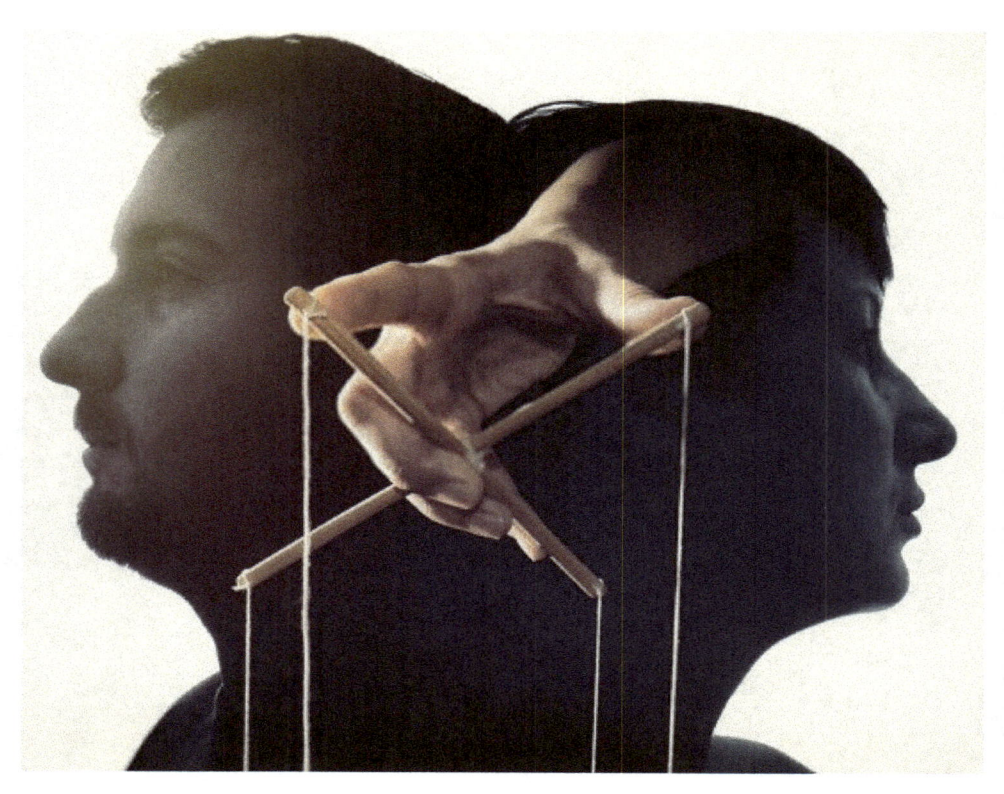

Legal Disclaimer

The information contained in this book and its contents is not designed to replace any form of medical or professional advice; and is not meant to replace the need for independent medical, financial, legal, or other professional advice or services that may be required. The content and information in this book have been provided for educational and entertainment purposes only.

The content and information contained in this book have been compiled from sources deemed reliable, and they are accurate to the best of the Author's knowledge, information, and belief. However, the Author cannot guarantee its accuracy and validity and therefore cannot be held liable for any errors and/or omissions. Further, changes are periodically made to this book as needed. Where appropriate and/or necessary, you must consult a professional (including but not limited to your doctor, attorney, financial advisor, or other such professional) before using any of the suggested remedies, techniques, and/or information in this book.

Upon using this book's contents and information, you agree to hold harmless the Author from any damages, costs, and expenses, including any legal fees, potentially resulting from the application of any of the information in this book. This disclaimer applies to any loss, damages, or injury caused by the use and application of this book's contents, whether directly or indirectly, whether for breach of contract, tort, negligence, personal injury, criminal intent, or under any other circumstance.

You agree to accept all risks of using the information presented in this book.

You agree that by continuing to read this book, where appropriate and/or necessary, you shall consult a professional (including but not limited to your doctor, attorney, financial advisor, or other such professional) before using any of the suggested remedies, techniques, or information in this book.

Table of Contents

Introduction *10*

Chapter 1: What is Gaslighting? *12*

   "Oh, Come On, You're Just Being Sensitive" 12

   Gaslighting At The Core **13**
     A Power Dynamic 14

   Gaslighting Signs **16**

   So, Is It A Mental Illness? **18**

Chapter 2: Narcissists and Gaslighting *21*

   What Is A Narcissist? **21**

   Narcissism And Gaslighting **24**
     The Art of Making Others Crazy 25
     Making People do What the Narcissist Wants 27

Chapter 3: The Cycle Of Gaslighting *32*

   Lies And Exaggeration **32**

   Repeat The Process **33**

   The Escalation **33**
     Wear The Victim Out 34

   Codependent Relationships **34**

   The False hope **35**

   Control Is The Goal **37**

Chapter 4: What Are The Symptoms Of
Gaslighting *39*
     Blatant Lies 39

   They'll Use What You Love As Ammo **40**

You Feel Worn Down Talking to them 41

Actions And Words Don't Match Up 42

Throws Positivity To Confuse You 43

You're Confused And Weak 44

Projection, Projection! 44

Others Are Against You 45

You Feel Crazy 46

Is Envious, And Thinks Everyone Is Lying 46

You Feel Yourself Start To Slowly Die 47

*Chapter 5: How Gaslighting Will Affect Your Life
IF You're Not Careful* 49

Memory Loss 49

You Feel Constantly Guilty 50

Isolation From Help 52

Self-Doubt 53

Social Life Issues 54

Difficulty Making Decisions 55

The Mental Health Side 56

A Refusal To Show Emotions 56

People Pleasing 57

Chapter 6: All About Cognitive Dissonance 60

The Origin Of This 60
The Strength Of The Dissonance 61

How Does This Relate To Gaslighting? 63

Some More Examples 65

How To Diffuse This? 66

Chapter 7: The Purpose of Gaslighting—What Is The Endgame? 68

All About Power 68

Control Until You Can't Do Anything....................................70

Start Small, Then Work Bigger 70

The Perfect Puppet Masters 72

Chapter 8: My Personal Experience With Gaslighting...77

Chapter 9: How To Cope With Those Who Gaslight You 81

Types Of Gaslighting 81

Understanding The Signs 82

7 Techniques To Disarm Narcissists So You're Not Under Their Control 85

Record It!...85

Don't Engage 85

Don't Take The Bait! 86

Set Boundaries 88

Empathize With Feelings 89

Stop Apologizing to Them! 90

Accepting That You Can't Change Them 91

Ask About Things That Interest Them................................92

The Final Choice: Leaving 93

Chapter 10: How To Recover From gaslighting .. 94

Understand What You're Dealing With 95

Get Out! 95

How To Handle Yourself 96

Surrounding Yourself With Love 97

Exercise Caution 99

Ignore The Motives 101

Chapter 11: How Gaslighting Is Used In Our Lives *103*

Gaslighting In Workspaces 103

Gaslighting In Politics And Society..................106

Gaslighting And Social Media 110

Co-Parenting And Divorce, How Gaslighting Is Used 112

Manipulative Parents And Gaslighting........... 115

Conclusion.. *118*

4

Introduction

Gaslighting. it's something that we hear about more often these days. In our world, abuse is something that is coming more and more to light. One type of abuse is, of course, gaslighting.

You have probably heard this term before. Maybe once, maybe many times. You might've heard about being gaslighted by someone in the past, or maybe you described your experience to someone, and they called it gaslighting.

So, what is it? Why is gaslighting such a problem? What could be done about it?

This is the question a lot of people have when it comes to gaslighting, simply because it's so toxic, and it can harm our own well-being. But, by understanding it, you can overcome the trials of the issues that come about from this, and work on bettering your own life.

In this book, we'll tell you how can change your life and improve it by recognizing the behaviors of gaslighting, how toxic they can be, and the best course of action on how to fight this.

We will go into below on the different aspects of gaslighting, and why it's something that you should be concerned about.

More and more people are coming forward about the abuse they've suffered in the past. Chances are, if you do one google search, you'll see many stories about people getting abused by past relations and the like, and you see the term gaslighting being thrown about.

So, what is it? How do you fight back when it happens? Well, I'll tell you the secrets on how to fight back when someone gaslights you, and how you can take control of your life again so you're not subject to the abuse. I'll give you the lowdown on the best means to combat this below, so you can understand what needs to be done.

By the end of this, you'll have the tools necessary to fight back against gaslighting, so you can be happier, and from there, take your life back as well.

Chapter 1

What Is Gaslighting?

So, before we begin, let's talk about what gaslighting is. it's something a lot of abusers love to do, and it's something many people, once they recognize the problem, want to do something about. Here, we'll highlight the basics of gaslighting, and why it's important to understand.

"Oh, Come On, You're Just Being Sensitive"

Have you heard these words before?

This is an example of gaslighting. If you've ever had an argument with someone, and they say "oh come on, you're being a baby/too sensitive/I never said that" then you've experienced firsthand what gaslighting is.

Gaslighting is an actual psychological term, but it means manipulation where the person who is trying to manipulate is working to make someone question their reality, the perception of it, and their recall. It is actually much more serious than you'd think, that's for sure.

It isn't just having someone question their reality though. Those who gaslight will continuously do this, with the ultimate purpose of making you question the validity of your own personalized understanding.

It is always a dangerous thing because it skewers your own reality.

Gaslighting At The Core

Gaslighting in practice is when someone denies what you said, making you out to be a liar, in order to force you to question your own reality. It is dangerous all the time since it forces you to let go of your own reality.

The offenses are usually small. For example, maybe you're upset someone didn't do something. You say this, and then they say, "you're just being sensitive, I would never do that." Sure, maybe they would not do it that one singular time, but what if they continuously do that.

Do you ever feel a bit upset and invalidated when you get your reality questioned this is a result of gaslighting? We all have our own reality and understanding of the situation. You may see it one way, and the person may see it another way.

The logical response to when something like this happens is to talk it out, work through it together, and understand that both of you have a different reality. But a manipulator won't care about anyone's reality but their own, so they'll do whatever it takes to squash the reality that you have.

Over time, you'll start to realize you're questioning your own life and intents. that's exactly what the manipulator wants out of this. The goal is for you to completely doubt yourself so that you'll end up in a state where you can't really negotiate when you want in life, or even your own terms, and instead, you're not focused, making inaccurate decisions, and in general have compromised a well-being.

Gaslighting doesn't' just happen between abusive boyfriends or girlfriends obviously. Anyone can gaslight. Your mom could gaslight you. Your coworkers could. Your asshole boss can. Oftentimes, people will not even realize that it's happening.

You can even argue that politicians do that. There are many times where people will confront Trump on his actions, and he'll immediately refute it, denying the reality with the intent of manipulating.

No matter where though, gaslighting is incredibly dangerous. People don't realize the effects this could have happened, and oftentimes, they may not do anything about it before it's too late.

we'll go into how to get out of an abusive situation where gaslighting is involved later, but for now, I want you to understand what gaslighting is at the core, and the signs of it too.

A Power Dynamic

The main reason why gaslighting happens is power. Oftentimes, the one who is manipulating has enough power that the one who is being targeted is too scared to change the relationship or step out because the threat of that relationship is there. There is also the threat of being seen as less than what you are to others, another major threat. If you notice that you're losing power in a relationship, oftentimes it may be gaslighting.

Marriage and family therapists so this a lot, and oftentimes, many people will struggle with being believed, since the manipulator loves to pay the strings in this whole situation. Many who are targets of gaslighting will as well change the opinions so that there isn't a conflict.

The gaslighted may not realize that they're being malicious either. It might be because of how they're raised or the like.

You will probably run into someone unintentionally gaslighting more often than not. Not every person who does this has ill intent, it might just be the way they act.

Now that you know a little bit about it, here are some important signs of gaslighting that you'll notice.

Gaslighting Signs

The signs of gaslighting are pretty simple to understand.

You see something that you don't understand, or maybe you don't like it. For example, let's say that Sally notices Joe is flirting with other girls. Sally tells Joe her thoughts.

Joe is a manipulator, or maybe he just thinks that he's just complimenting them. He tells her that he's just complimenting them, and to not be so overly sensitive, and to not worry about things.

Sally has this reality, and Sally gets told that basically, she's wrong and he's right and that she needs to stop worrying about things.

But you still question this. He says not to worry, not to be so "sensitive" and not to freak out and overreact. But you begin to notice that you're starting to question this.

It happens again. You question it again, and then Joe gets even more defensive, perhaps getting a bit rude and snappy with you. Oftentimes, at this point, Sally may begin to question herself, because this can be a "gaslight tango" which means that you're subtly starting to question yourself a lot.

Oftentimes the solution can be diffused of course, with communication and understanding why you're upset. For example, Sally could talk to Joe and explain her side of the story. But real manipulators may not totally get it, and oftentimes, they may criticize.

In abusive relationships, the one who is being manipulated will start to be squashed basically, here their own reality and understanding is basically nothing.

You see his parents as well. If you're someone who came from a family of strict parents, chances are you've probably experienced the effects of gaslighting. If you have a parent who is overly critical, chances are they will criticize because they believe it's "what's best" for them, but they may not even mean it in a bad way, but they come off as critical and just plain rude.

Many people oftentimes will do this with the intent of I'm just trying to help." but, of course, that help isn't a real help, it's actually a way to destroy your reality.

There are signs in particular that are important to understand to help you determine whether or not you're suffering from gaslighting, but some of the key signs to watch out for include the following:

- They are withholding information from you

- They counter your memory of an event

- They will block or divert to put the victim on another pathway

- They will trivialize the situation, and your feelings as well

- They will forget and deny, which means that they don't remember what happened, or they deny something that previously happened

if you start to notice these signs, then chances are, the person is gaslighting you. But we'll go into the actual signs that you have as a person who has suffered from gaslighting later on.

Gaslighters will sometimes start with something that is right and true, but you're sensitive to them pointing that out. That can set you off, and immediately hook you into their reality. it's a way for them to control what you're dealing with, and what you're going through.

For example, if you have a coworker who is claiming you don't work enough in the office, they may pull up that you complain about being tired because you switched birth control, which can be an actual thing. Yes, you may feel depressed due to medication changes and the like, but they may from there claim that you don't pull your weight. It may not even mean that you're not pulling your weight, they may just be doing this to be an asshole.

Gaslighting is manipulation, with the end goal to have you under their thumb. The instances range from complete denial of the incidents that have occurred to even doing things that disorient the victim. The origination from this was from a Patrick Hamilton play called Gaslight that was later adapted, which is where gas-fueled lights within their home are dimmed because the character searches in the bright attic at night. The main character in this convinces the wife that she's imagining that the lights in the attic are brighter and the house lights are dimmed. it's been used in both clinical studies, and literature that involves research as well, along with political commentary.

So, Is It A Mental Illness?

When it comes to gaslighting itself, it isn't a mental illness, however, it could be a sign of something more and a symptom of this.

However, those who have various personality disorders, such as narcissistic personality disorder, or even antisocial personality disorder might use gaslighting on others in order to change their reality in order to make it align with theirs. Psychologists have noticed that these types of people will deny that they do something even though you do have the proof. You know that said it, but they're completely denying it, so it makes you look bad.

Oftentimes, you see these with narcissists more than anything, since they love to charm those who are early on in the relationship, using pity party and victimizing I order to get what they want. If you reject their reality, they get very angry, and oftentimes, they will even go so far as stalking or following the person that they gaslight in order to completely squash their reality

those who have gaslit others have mostly superficial relationships, where they keep their friends at a distance and will only deal with them for a short period of time. They may see themselves in a different light when compared to people who see them, and they oftentimes will isolate those that they are close to from their friends and family to further keep them away from them.

Those who have antisocial personality disorder are also called sociopaths, which is a condition where people don't have any regard for right or wrong, and oftentimes ignore what other people are feeling as well. They oftentimes will antagonize and manipulate others with their indifference, and they'll have no remorse for their actions.

So, when someone who suffers from this gaslights others, they usually don't care what you have to say, and they don't really spend time trying to understand and forge the bond, but instead will continue to manipulate and keep quiet as they continue to change your reality.

Narcissists are a whole other can of worms, and we'll go into that in the next chapter.

But you need to understand that, if you're worried about being gaslit, then chances are, it probably has happened. If you notice that your reality and self-esteem keeps getting thwarted, that's a telltale sign of something bigger and something that's wrong.

So, how can you prevent this from becoming worse? We'll tell you how to handle someone like this in later chapters. But first, let's talk about narcissists, and how they fit into the picture.

Chapter 2

Narcissists and Gaslighting

So, we mentioned that narcissists have a hand in gaslighting, but what do they do/ they actually are huge manipulators, and they play a major role in changing the reality of others. Here, we'll discuss how they gaslight others, and why narcissists are bad news for many people.

What Is A Narcissist?

A narcissist is, by definition, someone that suffers from narcissistic personality disorder. Those who are narcissists tend to have an overly inflated sense of importance, and a need for admiration and attention in their relationships, and oftentimes don't have empathy for others.

Narcissists only care about themselves. They don't worry about you, or the guy next to you, but instead, they're only in it for their own benefit. However, they actually have an incredibly fragile ego that will shatter and is very vulnerable if they're hit with the smallest amount of criticism.

Narcissists are textbook manipulators, and they're not fun to deal with. This type of personality causes many issues in different areas of life, and you may run into one of these types without even realizing it. Typically, though, those who suffer from narcissistic personality disorder are unhappy in a general sense if they're not given the admiration they want. They may find all of their relationships unfulfilling, and others may not like being around these types of people.

So how does a narcissist come into your life? Well, those that suffer from this love to latch onto those that will hype them up, making them feel like they're special or unique, and in turn enhance their own self-esteem as a result. They may desire an immense amount of admiration and attention and have difficulty taking criticism in the slightest. They oftentimes see all criticism as defeat.

They are incredibly envious of your accomplishments, to the point where they will want to undermine them however, they can. This can be anything from snarky accomplishments regarding your success to underhanded comparing of others.

Narcissists love to use gaslighting too, but we'll get to that in a bit. For now, let's talk about how they will undermine you. If you do something great, they'll try to belittle it, saying that it's not worth it, and you need to do better. Sometimes, if the narcissist is a parent, they'll compare you to your sibling or someone else in the family. They oftentimes will try to belittle anything you do, turning you into a mess in response.

It's not good, and narcissists in general only care about themselves. Of course, many times only a small fraction of people are actual narcissists, but in general, there are more male narcissists than female narcissists, and you oftentimes will run into them when you're dealing with bosses, coworkers, or even people you may be friends with or date.

But, how can these people use gaslighting? Well, they do so in a very crafty manner.

Narcissism And Gaslighting

Narcissists love to use gaslighting. In fact, it's their favorite, most preferred tool of gaslighting. Why is that? Well, it's because it's the perfect way to make you think you're crazy, to completely undermine what you think is right, and to basically tell you that your way of thinking is wrong.

Remember, gaslighting is a very sneaky way of making you feel like your reality is so distorted to the point where the person will question their own sanity or even their memory. Their goal is to make it so that they're right, you're wrong, and that's all they want from this.

The goal is to make you think you're crazy, which we'll get to in a bit. There are other tools narcissist will use, but gaslighting is their bread and butter.

"Oh, I never said that."

"Oh, you're remembering it wrong, clearly you should get yourself checked out."

If you've ever heard those two things before from someone, you're dealing with a Grade A Narcissist.

Gaslighting is used by narcissists because it's how they love to hide the abuse they're inflicting upon you. In essence, gaslighting is lying straight to your face, with one singular goal in mind, to be the ones in control, the center of attention, and you're nothing.

Basically, every time a narcissist gaslights you, they're basically completely ruining what sense of reality you have, making you realize that it's nothing, and they're everything.

They want to break you down slowly but surely. Memory is one of the easiest ways to do this. Why is that? Well, it's because they know that if you can't remember things right, you're not going to be able to trust yourself, distorting your own personal perception and reality that comes with this.

So yes, it does happen like that, and the goal is for you to completely rely on the abuser to tell you what's real so that over time the abuser is the one in control of your life, the one taking the reins here in the game.

The Art of Making Others Crazy

This is something that a lot of narcissists use gaslighting for. Remember, gaslighting is basically refuting anyone's reality, making it so that what they think is right really isn't.

When a narcissist gaslights, they will put down and refute anything that you say. They will do this to make it sound like they're the ones who are right when in reality, it's their own mind games.

It's all a game for a narcissist. They want to make it so that your reality isn't correct. While you might believe that you're right, the narcissist will tell you right away that you aren't. Over time as you continue to be refuted by the narcissist, you start to doubt your own reality. You start to think that you're the bad guy when in reality, it's just your narcissist playing games.

When a narcissist gaslights, they can change the view that you have of people, in general, being good. You might think that people, in general, are good, which they are, but oftentimes, if you have a narcissist in your life, this person will not protect your feelings. Someone you may think is good turns out to be bad, and someone that you thought was bad turns out to be good since that's how the narcissist wants you to think.

A narcissist will use gaslighting for the sole reason of, they know exactly how to manipulate you. You start to doubt your own reality, and over time, you start to wonder if maybe you are crazy. After all, after so often, you may wonder if you're not right in the head. But remember, more often than not, narcissists were the cause of this, and they're the reason why you think this way.

Lots of times narcissists will start by buttering you up, making you feel loved and appreciated since that's what they want you to believe. After a while, they will start to, over time, start to treat you like crap. When you call them out on it, they'll start to mask their true feelings, and you'll be seeing a totally different side.

But the reality is, that mask that they put on is, of course, their mask, and the abusive nature that they've had till now is their true form.

It can slowly erode the trust that you've had in yourself. After all, you thought that you could trust this person to always be there for you, and you start to notice they're nowhere near as good. Ut, after a bit, you realize that they're actually garbage, and you start to see how they really are.

They will tell you what you think is what happened isn't what happened, but that's actually how it is. But of course, in the world of the narcissist, they'll only make you believe what they think is right.

Gaslighting basically takes away everything that you think is correct, which then causes you to follow what they think is the way when in reality, they're manipulating you.

You're basically forced to believe that you're crazy, or if you don't think you're crazy, that the abuser is wrong, but you can't stand up for yourself. They will either manipulate you until you believe you're wrong and they are right or drive you to the point of insanity.

Gaslighters and narcissists love this. Because they know that, once you discount your own personal beliefs enough, you'll start to really think that you are crazy, and slowly start to believe them.

Making People do What the Narcissist Wants

This is done because most of the time, when you start to discount how a narcissist acts, they will immediately gaslight you, saying that it didn't happen this way.

You notice your narcissist abuser is acting gross and mean, and you notice that for example, they're flirting with other girls. They totally are, and you call them out on it, but they will immediately say that isn't the case, tell you that you're crazy, that you're making stuff up, and basically tell you whatever you saw was wrong.

Deep down, you know what the truth is. That the actions you saw were valid, but over time, this person will continuously tell you that you're crazy, that you didn't really hear or say what was said.

You start to doubt your own reality, and you begin to wonder if you remembered everything right. Perhaps you didn't catch the other person flirting with girls. You start to go silent on it. When in reality, your narcissist was totally doing that, didn't come clean, and now this person is seeing girls, and every time you call them out on that, and their own trust and validity, basically tells you that you're insane, and you're wrong.

You stop fighting the narcissist after a while. You notice that every time you fight them there really is no end to it and the fact that you're constantly told that you're crazy every time you do isn't a good thing for you either. So, what do you do from here?

The answer is most people tend to give in to their abusers.

Instead of doing what they feel is right, which is calling out the abuser and recognizing the toxic traits, you start to do exactly what the abuser wants. Because whenever you're gaslit, you start to feel like you're wrong, and that the narcissist is right. You're pretty much duped into believing that the narcissist is the right person, and you're wrong, making your reality practically nothing.

If you let this continue, you're basically feeding the supply of narcissism that the other person craves. You may start to perceive things wrong, and oftentimes, it gets to the point where you swore it was that way, but maybe your stuff is gone, because the narcissist hides it, and then they claim that you're irresponsible, and not worthy of trust. They will then tell you that you're wrong and crazy, and they'll start to make others think that you're crazy.

They will even pit others against you to isolate others. Oftentimes, they'll try to put you against others, so you drop them, and the only person in your life is the narcissist. They'll make up lies, and you can't really trust anyone but the person who is gaslighting you.

When in reality, the one who is gaslighting you is the last person that you should be trusting!

Gaslighters don't really realize just how harmful they are, or maybe they do. They will start to make you question even the most random of strangers. You might start to brush off someone's actions as being harmless, but the gaslighted will call it flirting, and soon, you start to attack anyone who comes at you.

Have you ever seen this? Maybe you've experienced it. Where you will hear about how someone was looking at you the wrong way, you start to grow weary and angry with the other person, and over time, those relationships break down since you think they can't be trusted. When in reality, it's the narcissist who can't be trusted, because they're the one putting you in this direction.

A narcissist will hurt literally everyone in your life, pit you against the friends and family that you have so that you're distracted from what the narcissist is really doing, which is feeding you harmful lies.

It's a messy situation and not something that most of us want to deal with.

So yes, a narcissist will use gaslighting. It's the prime tool of narcissist because they know that they can bend others to the will that they have, making it very easy to manipulate them, and that's why many narcissists will smile at you with a warm, fake smile, and then stab you in the back whenever you turn around, or put your family and friends against you, so the only person you can really rely on, is the narcissist themselves

It's their main tool, their bread, and butter, and you can understand why that is in this chapter. Now that you know, let's dive a bit deeper into what exactly narcissists will do to you, and how it causes major issues later on.

Chapter 3

The Cycle Of Gaslighting

Here's the truth of it: gaslighting happens in a cycle. It's a form of manipulation, along with brainwashing that's used to make victims doubt who they are, and ultimately lose their sense of self-worth, and also perception and of course, identity.

Usually in most milder situations, there is a weird power dynamic that isn't equal in relationships, where the one who is experiencing gaslighting is subject to the actions of when one who is doing so, and oftentimes, if at the very worst, it can be almost like severe mind control, and not healthy for anyone.

There are seven stages though for the most part that most who experience gaslighting go through, and below, we'll discuss what they are.

Lies And Exaggeration

This is usually the first step after you've been buttered up enough, usually with praise and fake words. The gaslighter will now make some negative comments about the one who is being gaslighted, and usually, it's about how you're inadequate, or some fault in you. This is based on generalized opinions, rather than a subjective, verified fact, and thereby will put the one who is being gaslighted onto the defensive. Usually, this is very exaggerated and awkward as well, such as the mom getting mad at the daughter for putting items on the checkout counter before she does. She may claim she "hates it" but when prompted will usually make up some fairy tale lie, and usually it doesn't have much bearing.

Repeat The Process

Usually, this isn't done just one. Although, I wish it was. Usually, they won't do it once, because they know that one time won't be enough. In fact, they will continue to do it because they know that it's psychological warfare since the falsehoods continue to be created in order to be on the offensive, so they can stay in control. You can't do it once, but instead, you do it multiple times, in order to be dominant in the relationships that you have.

The Escalation

Every time someone who gaslights someone is challenged, they won't back down. In fact, the gaslighted will escalate everything further whenever there is a chance to challenge it, since they will double and triple down on the attacks, so if you refute it once, you'll from there be refuted again and again, and they'll make sure that they will make it worse and worse each time.

Every time you try to blame something on them, they'll refuse it, no matter what it is that they do. They will from there also refute any evidence that there with either final, false claims in order to misdirect the person, and also blame. That's right, you'll be blamed for whatever it is that they would do.

What's wild about this one, is that some people who do this are so forceful with believing that they did no wrong, that they were the good guys in this, that you could watch them outright in the act, and from there, they will try to refute you. So, if you say that you saw your partner with another person, they will refute it by saying it didn't happen or even get to the point where they will call you names regarding it.

They will make sure that it's done again and again, and it will only get worse for the victim as time goes on.

Wear The Victim Out

They will do this, continuing on the offensive so that you're worn out. The gaslighted will wear down the victim over time. The victim will be incredibly discouraged, pessimistic, resigned, debilitated, and also doubt themselves completely. The victim will start to realize that they may be the ones in the wrong at this point, and start to question their own sense of reality, and even their own identity and perception.

This does go on for a while. This is something that happens a lot, and it's something that a lot of people will experience over time. They will feel this struggle simply because they know that as they continue to fight with their gaslighted, it only gets worse.

It's even more so when the gaslighted is someone that will also be a narcissist too. They will do it because they know that they can slowly start to get the other person's attention, and they will do this because they can wear the victim down. That's where the next step comes in.

Codependent Relationships

This is a relationship that is based on psychological and emotional reliance on another person. Essentially, you're basically relying on the other person almost completely, to the point where you can't really think for yourself, and you have to emotionally and mentally rely on another person.

This isn't a healthy relationship, and in fact, is incredibly toxic. To the point where the gaslighted will start to make the one who is being gaslighted constantly insecure and anxious about this. They will, with this as well, make the person unable to rely on anyone else but the gaslighted, which will pull the other person by the strings.

The gaslighted is the one in charge here, the head honcho tat has the power to grant approval, respect, security, and safety to the one who is being gaslighted. The one who is manipulating often times has the power and will at times be so strong with this that they will try their hardest to take it away. Codependent relationships are of course, not healthy, and they rely on marginalization and vulnerability in order to make it so that one of them isn't able to ever escape, and must rely on the second person in order to get anywhere.

The False hope

This is a manipulation tactic where the gaslighted will sometimes be a bit nicer to the one who is being gaslighted, allow for someone to have superficial kindness, mindfulness of their actions, or even a bit of moderation, but that's actually a false hope. This is in place because the victim is then meant to think that hey, the other person isn't all that bad, right? After all, this is definitely something that could be worse.

But, that's actually not the case. That's a false hope. The intent behind it is to make the person think that it's worth staying here. In reality, that's just a show that they put on. They are in reality not going to change.

The purpose of this is to deceive you. After all, they know what they are doing, and it's a calculated move that is supposed to instill complacency within the victims that are there.

They want you to put your guard down, and if you do, that's opening you up to more abuse. They want you to put your guard down before you're gaslit once again. This also reinforces codependency, because you feel like you need them.

Sure, they may be nice for a minute, and they may get you things and do nice things, but you shouldn't believe it.

It's a temporary move in order to make you vulnerable to the next bout of gaslighting. Because, as we've said before, they won't stop. They won't ever give up until of course, they have complete control.

Control Is The Goal

Control is the goal, and it's a very extreme level of control. This isn't just that they control a couple of things in your life. No, those who use gaslighting will control everything that they can. The ultimate goal of someone who gaslights like this is to dominate, take control, and take advantage of the other person, or in some cases, the whole society that's there. Once this is maintained and intensified, it will only continue on.

You've been beaten down so much already by this person too, that it's no wonder why people will think that this is the only way.

But it's not. However, for those who are victims of gaslighting, they are subject to the coercion, lies, and occasional false hopes that are put in place.

The one who is being manipulated suffers the most. It's the fact that all you'll ever feel is insecurity, fear, and doubt from everything that's happened. The one who gaslights you will exploit you whenever possible and the argument is only personal gain and power.

Narcissists will fully control your life, and one of the results of a narcissistic gaslighted is doubting everything that you do. This isn't just a couple of things; no this is everything that you do in life and everything that happens in your life too. Once you start down this path, it can wreck your self-confidence, and that's something that the narcissistic gaslighted wants.

In relationships, this often translates to the person being under the thumb of the one who gaslights, always having to follow the instructions of the other person and making it worse for you as well. In relationships, there is very little freedom in life, and you'll realize that, with this as well, you're never going to get out until you do the right thing.

We will go over how to exit a relationship that has gaslight in it, but we'll also go over a few of the symptoms of gaslighting that'll happen if you're not careful, and what will happen if you're still in this position in the next chapter.

Gaslighting is a cycle of control, and you shouldn't ever believe that the abuser will get better. Abusers don't learn, they don't get better, and you'll only be on the path to hurt and pain if you continue with them. Save yourself the heartache, and instead, do what's right for you.

Start to take control of your life, of your wellness, and start to do something about it now, before it gets worse for you.

Chapter 4

What Are The Symptoms Of Gaslighting

So, what are some symptoms of gaslighting that you can either see, experience, or what you need to be careful about? Here, we'll highlight the symptoms of gaslighting that you need to be careful about.

Blatant Lies

This is one that you should always be careful of. Lies are something the person who is gaslighting you loves to tell. After all, they know that they are blatant lies. Why are they so blatant though? Well, essentially this is setting the bar on which they're going to work. For example, if you start to hear lies from them, maybe you'll start to give in. you will start to wonder if anything they do say is true. You know it's a lie, but every time you try to refute it, they simply just completely ignore what you say, or turn the blame on you.

It oftentimes also comes with denial. They will deny everything that's done until the day that they die, even if they know that you have proof. They will oftentimes act like they would do something, and they do it, but then when you catch them, they completely deny it. Even if you have proof, they'll say that you're making it up, you're crazy, and you're lying.

But are you lying?

Nope. But they will fight you tooth and nail until you give up. The goal that they have in hand is to make sure that they are the ones in charge, and the goal of this is complete control, so your reality is completely tarnished so that you'll accept literally everything that's said from their lips. Event Of course, if it isn't true.

They'll Use What You Love As Ammo

This is seen a lot of times when you're dealing with a gaslighted who a parent to a kid is. They love to use the kids as ammo. They may do this with other things too. If you love your pets, they use that as ammo. If you have a family who matters a lot, they'll make sure to know how important it is to you, and it's one of the first things they'll choose to attack.

If you have a family, maybe they'll say that you shouldn't be so close to your family, or that your family takes pity on you. When it comes to kids, they'll outright say how you're not worthy of having them, and they will say that you shouldn't have them.

They want to attack you below the belt. They will go after the negative traits that you have and tell you that you suck, that you do everything wrong, and that you're worthless.

Why do they do this? Chances are, they want to knock you down a peg or two to the point where you accept everything ate abuser is saying as reality. You will start to wonder if you are because they will target all of your sensitive points, even if you don't think they will.

You Feel Worn Down Talking to them

If you feel this way when talking to people, chances are you might be getting gaslit. This is why gaslighting is so insidious, because they know that they will wear you down over time.

The comments will be snide, they'll say things here and there, all of it will be insidious, but the goal is to slowly chip away your own fortitude, to break you down.

And what's sad is, it works.

Even those who have the strength, power, and ability, and are even self-aware of their own actions and feelings can be sucked into this trap, which is why it's so scary. It's kind of like that analogy of a frog in a frying pan.

Have you ever heard of that one? The analogy is that frogs are put into a frying pan, but the heat within it is very slowly increased, to the point where the frog won't notice until it's cooked to a crip—when it's too late.

You often won't even know you're being abused in this fashion until it's too late, which is the scariest part of gaslighting, and it's a reason why many abusers will continue to do this for years down the line.

Actions And Words Don't Match Up

Remember the phrase actions speak louder than words? Well, when dealing with someone who loves to gaslight, you need to pay attention to their actions, rather than their words.

They will do things ut then oftentimes will be in complete opposition to what they actually say.

"Oh, I would never talk to her and hurt you dear"—Goes off and is seen with other girls.

"I do love you dear"—Will completely belittle your life

"I do care about you and want you to live your own life"— Will take away their daughter's clothing and other aspects of their style.

Usually, this is seen mostly with abusive boyfriends, or abusive parents, where they will say one thing and then do another thing, and they oftentimes will end up continuously making it so that they are not doing what they should be doing.

Of course, the goal here is to confuse you and make you wonder if actually there is a true self of this person, and if they are who they say they are.

Throws Positivity To Confuse You

This is something a lot of people will not realize will happen. They will throw positivity occasionally in order to confuse you. They'll be nothing but complete assholes to you, always making it so that you're nothing, putting you down and making you feel bad, will tell outright lies and say that you're crazy but every now and then, they'll throw a little sprinkle of positive reinforcement, with the intention of trying to confuse you.

They will cut you down, and tell you that you're worthless, but then will randomly praise you for the actions that you do.

Why would they do that? Wouldn't it be better if you were just put down? Nope, because the goal here is to confuse you, and make you feel uneasy.

They want you to think that the abuser "isn't so bad, right?" and you start to let the abuser get away with things because they're nice to you every once in a while. They will oftentimes try to make you question your reality, and it works. You oftentimes will look at what you were given praise for, and you can usually trace it back to it benefitting the gaslighted.

This is especially true in narcissistic gaslighting relationships. You have a narcissistic mother, you're constantly belittled, torn down, and oftentimes are basically made to be nothing. But occasionally, there is that small inkling of "hey, you're not shit" that they give to you. This is only because you did something that they were happy about or something that benefitted them. They oftentimes will also try to put in a little bit of their own little two cents into it too, saying that it was totally them who helped out, and that's the reason why you were actually so successful.

You're Confused And Weak

Confusion is the name of the game. Why is that? Well, confusion is how you weaken a person.

They know that stability is what people want. They want the status quo, the normalcy that goes along with this. However, they want to completely unroot that and make you question everything and anything that happens. And of course, we have a natural tendency to look at the entity that will help you feel more stable and view them as someone that they should turn to when things get rough.

Who's the person that they turn to though? You guessed it, the one who is gaslighting them.

They want to make it so that you're confused, you have nowhere else to go, and the only solution is your gaslighted. They don't' want you to feel stable and secure, and they'll do everything possible to make sure that you're not.

Projection, Projection!

Projection is the bread and butter of these types. We'll go a little bit more into this later on, but they do experience the cognitive dissonance and projection that most other abusive and bad people feel.

They will claim that you're cheating, that you're stealing items, and oftentimes, they will basically claim that you're doing something.

When you start to get accused, you'll find yourself, and as you try to defend yourself, it becomes about you. Sometimes, they'll even try to confuse you and say that you're the one who is doing everything, creating a guilt complex within you.

But, who is the real cheater here? Who is the real abuser?

You guessed it, the gaslighted.

They will immediately start to blame you with the full intent of taking the blame and pinning it somewhere else. They are the ones cheating. But, every time you talk to them about it or confront them, it immediately will be turned back to you, one for one.

Others Are Against You

Don't think that they are just going for you at this point and only want to squash you. No, they are really amazing at manipulating those that they know will be near them no matter what, and they'll use them against you.

For example, if a narcissistic mother is gaslighting you, chances are, she's got the "golden child" that can do no wrong, that is perfect, that she can use immediately manipulate and use against you. They will make comments like that the other person knows that you're incorrect, or they will say that you're worthless and you aren't to be trusted. However, they might have not even told others about you, or maybe that other person has never said that, but of course, they are lying and will continually lie.

Gaslighters love to use this tactic in order to make it so that you don't know who friend or foe is, and who you can rely on. The goal is of course for you to realize that there is nobody and that you need to be with the gaslighted.

And of course, that gives them exactly what they want, and more control as well. They want you to go back to the gaslighted, and you'll realize that with this as well, there is a lot that happens as a result of this, where you may feel like your family hates you.

Sometimes, narcissistic mothers or stepparents will turn one side of the family and will say that this person hates you and never wants to see you. But that really isn't the case. In fact, when you reconnect with them, they might tell you that was never the case, and they were wrong.

And Of course, you can thank your gaslighted for that.

You Feel Crazy

They may tell you straight that you're crazy, or they may tell other people that you're crazy.

This is one of their primary tools because done in a manner that's incredibly dismissive. They will sometimes in a matter-of-fact manner say that this person is crazy, that they shouldn't be trusted, that you shouldn't listen to them. The gaslighted as they utter this know that you're going to not question it.

Of course, if the other person questions it and asks you, they won't believe you, since they know that when you say that the gaslighted is abusive, it's out of your control, and it's a really good technique.

Is Envious, And Thinks Everyone Is Lying

If you notice that the other person is saying that they're jealous of the gaslighted, or maybe they say that everyone else is a liar, then it's high time you got out of there and realized what you're dealing with.

The concept behind doing this is such: once you tell the one who is being abused that everyone else is a liar, guess what it does again? It makes you question your own reality of course! You oftentimes will never know someone that has the courage (or recklessness) to do this sort of thing, and obviously, it's your gaslighted so it has to be true right? Well, it's not. They will say that everyone is lying, that everyone else has it wrong, and the gaslighted is the only one with the right information.

"Oh don't listen to your friends, they're obviously lying. They don't really know me."

"Your grandma is a crazy bitch, she obviously has it wrong, and she's losing her sanity, so don't listen to her."

"It's for your own good not to listen to your mom. She's an asshole, and she constantly lies about everything."

They will claim that other people are liars, and they can do no wrong, but the reality of it is, you're the one who is dealing with a grade A liar, and you're the one who has to deal with the fallout from that.

So yes, gaslighters will lie in order to turn you on these people, since of course, they're clearly all liars, right?

You Feel Yourself Start To Slowly Die

I'm not always talking physically with this one. But this is one of the worst signs of gaslighting that you start to feel. You start to slowly start to realize that you're turning into someone completely different.

This is seen more than anything else in how confident you are. Victims of gaslighting seem to lose all of their confidence, and what's scary, is even the most confident of individuals can become a hollow husk of the person that they used to be. And what's even scarier, is they might not even realize that it's happening.

Victims will start to diminish in terms of their own reality, so they will only act in ways that benefit the gaslighter.

This is why some people who are victims of narcissistic abuse sometimes take on the traits of the abuser. Some people who are gaslighted by others will take on the traits of the other person or may even become yes men because they don't know what else to do.

It's sad when this happens, and it's why when if you get away from your narcissistic abuser, you can start to feel more alive, more like yourself, and so much happier in the long run.

These are the telltale signs of gaslighting, and if you notice that there is gaslighting happening, you need to start doing something about it. It can be scary, but it's possible to leave, especially if your own sanity is at stake.

Chapter 5

How Gaslighting Will Affect Your Life IF You're Not Careful

Remember that you can get away from the abuse, but there are things that can happen if you're not careful, if you continue to stay in the presence of someone who gaslights you, and who abuses you.

What can happen though/ let's talk about what can happen if you continue to suffer at the hands of a gaslighter?

Memory Loss

This is what's so scary about gaslighting. When you experience gaslighting after a while, sometimes you'll start to feel so guilty and have a lot of self-doubts that you'll tend to forget things that happened. You may not know why it happened, and not remember things that happened between those time periods. Some people will even experience the abuser accusing them of something that happened, but they're unable to actually remember what happened.

Sometimes, what's scary about gaslighting is when you experience that, over a long period of time, you'll begin to realize that you can't remember the exact situations, because your mind and reality is completely skewered. You'll start to realize that you can't remember things that the abuser would accuse you of.

Sometimes, the abuser would accuse you of things that you're doing, but you don't remember doing them, and this, in turn, will lead you to wonder whether or not you did something. You'll definitely start to realize this as well when you getaway.

Sometimes, they'll claim you're abusive, and how you hurt them, but you literally can't remember why. You oftentimes will try very hard to remember the abuse and trauma, but you can't.

Another type of way you can lose your memory with this is blanking on various things. When you're gaslit, you start to feel your reality starts to change, and you start to become an effect of the abuser that's there. However, sometimes after gaslighting happens, you can't remember all of the trauma you went through.

Perhaps it's a defensive mechanism, or maybe it's just your brain trying to blackout everything terrible that happened to you. But, you won't remember things. Your memory starts to become less and less, to the point where it becomes a struggle to remember it all.

You may walk around with really bad brain fog too. Abusers love to skewer your sense of reality, so when they do this, you can't remember things and your brain becomes a foggy mess as a result of this.

You Feel Constantly Guilty

One-way narcissistic abusers take you down is making you feel guilty constantly. It isn't a pity party "oh woe is me" concept, it's more of they will make you feel bad for even existing. That's the problem with narcissistic abusers. They will make sure that you feel guilty, constantly terrible, and you're the one at fault.

Narcissistic abusers will throw jabs at you, telling you how you're nothing. They will also say that you're just worthless, a piece of trash, and you're constantly not allowed to be anything more. That's the problem with many abusers. They will oftentimes make you feel guilty, to the point where depression, even suicidal tendencies start to come up.

You wonder if you're the one to blame for everything. You start to feel like you're the one at fault, when you may not be. Even when you're out of the situation and away from it, even years down the road, it can haunt you, like a ghost that hasn't been exorcised yet.

You feel bad for even being alive and that's because your narcissistic abuser has taken you to such a lower level that you don't know what to do with yourself other than to think that hey, you are the one to blame, and you are worthless. But of course, that isn't the case.

Isolation From Help

This is what's scary about narcissistic abusers. Remember, they will claim that you're the one who is crazy, that others are lying, that you're not the one who is right here. They will tell you that you should only believe them, and never anyone else.

Over time, when you're with an abuser like this, you can develop a Stockholm syndrome, where you know that you need to get away, but you can't. you isolate yourself from help, and oftentimes, even after you get ut, you can't really get the help that you need.

That's because you don't trust other people. They are all liars, remember? Your abuser would tell you that, and even if you've managed to leave, that can hang around in your head.

That's why, when people who have been gaslighted leave their abusers, they sometimes can't trust other people. They don't know if they ever can and are scared to do so because of what their abuser did in the past.

Self-Doubt

Self-doubt stems from how you were treated by your gaslighters. The goal of those who gaslight is to make the other person feel worthless like their own thoughts and reality don't matter. Sometimes, those who have been gaslighted will hallucinate, and sometimes they'll see things that aren't there in order to make the gaslighted happy.

But, the self-doubt extends past that. When someone how has been gaslighted all their lives finally leaves, they are often scared of what's next. They've been living with the reality of their abuser for so long that they don't know how to wrench themselves away.

This causes self-doubt. It's the doubt of oneself, the doubt of what's really out there and the doubt of their own reality. And boy is it terrible for you.

Self-doubt makes you second-guess everything that you do from here on out. After all, when you've been told you're worthless all your life, you probably will think that everything you do is worthless. But it isn't, that's just the gaslighted talking in your head.

Gaslighters love to do this because they know that, if you are continually taken down, if you ever do leave, you'll never really be yourself again, because you're scared to be. You'll be scared of expressing yourself, of being who you are, and you'll realize that, if you continue with this mindset, it will only make things worse from here on out, and for many, it can be a deadly action that can help erase who you really are.

This type of self-doubt can stifle creativity too and dreams as well, so remember that. You may feel like you should do something, but then, because you've been gaslighted in the past, you shy away from doing so. Oftentimes, this type of abuse will stunt your own creativity, and there is a reason why many people encourage those who have been gaslit to escape while they can.

Social Life Issues

Sometimes, gaslighting does affect your social life. The abuser will try their very hardest to keep the one who is gaslighted away from their friends, or even family too. The constant lying and saying they are bad people will happen. Lots of times, those who have suffered from gaslighting might end up never seeing their family until years down the road. This is something that can happen for a very long time.

What's scary as well, is that the person might end up completely isolating themselves from anyone, only relying on the abuser and nothing else. It can make the person feel like they're not capable of being loved, and also make the person feel like they're not stable, which is the scariest part about it.

For many people who have suffered the effects of gaslighting, they oftentimes will feel their confidence tank as well, since nobody seems to care about them or make an effort to go see them when in reality they're oftentimes being forced away from those relationships.

And what's scary, is that this can last a long time, even after you've left the relationship. Many who have been gaslighted in the past will not go back to their former friends and family right away, due to the effects of it. There is a reason why people will make sure that they seek out the help that they need, so they can reconnect with the person that they missed right away.

Difficulty Making Decisions

Decision Making was done all from the abuser, and not very much from the person who was gaslighted. So, if you've experienced a bit of hesitation in decisions and have a history of abuse, you can probably thank gaslighting for that.

Decisions were left to the other person, and whenever you did make decisions, it was oftentimes seen as wrong, or incorrect to do. So why make decisions then?

That's why many, who have suffered from gaslighting in the past, can doubt the decisions that they make, from there, may not believe what they're doing is right.

This can lead to anxiety disorders in many cases. You're afraid of making decisions because whenever you did, you were always told that they were wrong. You were abused so much that you don't know what to do about anything anymore, so decision making is very hard for those who've suffered from narcissistic abuse. Sometimes, this might seem like a couple of things are hard to decide, and other times, some people will just have trouble making any decision period.

Gaslighting can also make someone feel like their feelings and emotions don't matter, so they oftentimes have to choose what to do from a distanced viewpoint. So, instead of deciding from the heart, and in a way that'll validate and help you, they're swimming in a pool of anxiety and stress, that isn't fun for anyone who suffers from this.

The Mental Health Side

There is also the mental health side of the effects of gaslighting. We did go over anxiety, but that's due to the confusion that the person makes the one who is being gaslit feel. The one who is being gaslit oftentimes doesn't know what's right and wrong, and they fear to do things. This can be a small occurrence, or this can be a major issue in their life that does need to be discussed.

The one who is suffering from being gaslit may also feel a lot of hopelessness, along with self-esteem issues. This can also lead to depression, and oftentimes, people who are survivors of this oftentimes still feel like life is hopeless, that their feelings don't matter, and that they should never talk about it.

Depression is another major issue, since many times, being taken down so low for so long can make the person feel like it's not worth the energy as well.

PTSD is another one. After all, you were in a traumatic and abusive situation. The shock and stress from that person's actions still linger there, and it commonly develops from this.

Finally, codependency is something that can develop from this too. That's because you've been living a life where you had that type of relationship, and it can make you feel like you have to rely on others.

A Refusal To Show Emotions

This is a big one. This is due to the fact that survivors will always be on guard, always looking for the manipulation that's in any situation. Oftentimes, this can lead to people not trusting themselves, or trusting others either, and people do describe those who have suffered from this as always on guard.

They refuse to be vulnerable, for a good reason. They don't want to be hurt like that again. However, the problem with that, while it's a notable reason, it can be a problem for some people, since they'll refuse to show manipulation to the point where future relationships are stained, and they may have trouble holding a relationship because of this.

It does happen. Lots who suffer from this may even refuse to show emotions to others, staying single for a long time because they'd rather not be hurt, and would rather not experience what they did again.

It's a problem because they may really like someone, but the idea of being that vulnerable is something they don't think they can do, and sometimes, they will refuse to really step forward and do anything about it, and they will always keep everyone at a distance.

Some may not see this as a problem, but when the interpersonal relationships come in, it can be devastating for them.

People Pleasing

On the other side of the coin, some people will become validation hungry after they've been abused for so long. That's due to the fact that they've been forced to experience this for so long that they don't know how to do anything else but look for validation, although it may not be in the healthiest of ways.

People-pleasing isn't a good trait to have. It can make them outright refuse to change certain behaviors because they know that it pleases others. They might be seen as attention-seeking, and they will try to keep others around, even if it means sacrificing a little bit of themselves in the process.

These are the people that do harmful things to themselves, and to others, for the sole purpose of validation, but the problem is, this opens them up to further abuse. Not everyone will sympathize with the person who is recovering from abuse, and not everyone will understand. Some people will, in fact, use this person in order to further themselves. Some abusers might even go so far as to try and manipulate this person again, and from there, they become the target of another's abuse.

Abusers will look for people like this since they're incredibly easy to manipulate, they will jump right in and make this person a target. So the person who suffers from this really doesn't actively get away from the abuse, but instead, they're the subject of another abuser's attacks, whether it be someone similar or otherwise.

This is the other side of the coin, the side most people don't realize does happen if you're not careful and end up getting caught in the web of this. It can be just as bad as not showing emotion at all and tends to be worse.

That isn't to mention all of these aren't problems. They sure are, and people don't realize that if the abuse isn't taken care of or handled, it will only get harder for the person who is being gaslighted to actually break free, and do something about it. That's why many people need to understand that, in order to actively create the best situation for themselves, they need to take the abuse into their own hands and start doing something about it.

It can be very hard to escape, but it is possible. We'll talk about this. The recovery is a long road simply because the abuse basically has uncertainty at the beginning of it.

People will grow up and mistrust everything that they feel, and oftentimes, recovering from this can take a long time. But we'll tell you how to get away, and how you can use this book to escape your abuser's actions and feel better about recovering from it all.

Chapter 6

All About Cognitive Dissonance

One part of abusers is the fact that they will use cognitive dissonance in order to assert control. Here, we'll highlight what this is, and how it relates to gaslighting, and what you can do about it.

Usually, this term is used to explain discomfort and feelings that happen when your beliefs are against what others are bringing forward, or there is no information given to you. Oftentimes, the goal of this is consistency in perceptions and attitudes, so when vie s that you believe are true are challenged, or what you do isn't what others think, sometimes, people will make sure that the dissonance is reduced, or change this in order to make it so that the issue isn't there anymore.

It might seem like a good thing, but it's not. The most common way to describe it is of course, "explaining things away." You see this with abusers a lot, and there is a reason why this is the bread and butter of your abusers.

The Origin Of This

The term was originally put forward by a psychologist named Leon Festinger, who first proposed this since this is a theory that people will use in order to keep the consistency internal. This is because they want to keep the behaviors and beliefs consisting.

The idea behind this is harmony. If there are conflicting beliefs or even ideas, this leads to disharmony. It's a natural part of life to avoid disharmony, and instead, encourage harmony in life.

Festinger, later on, wrote a book called *A Theory of Cognitive Dissonance* which was published in 1957. The idea behind this is that it's an antecedent condition which then will lead towards a dissonance reduction. They will do an activity in order to reduce the dissonance that is going on. It's a very different motivation from what others deal with, but it's powerful. This is something that's also influenced by other factors as well.

The Strength Of The Dissonance

Not all dissonance is equal, that's something you'll learn right away. This depends on certain factors that are important. Below are the factors that usually control the cognitive dissonance in something, and why it matters.

- Cognitions that have a more personal idea to them have more dissonance, and this includes your self-beliefs
- The ratio of dissonance is based on the clashing and consonant or harmonious thoughts, and you are trying to strive for perfect balance, no matter what
- The beliefs that you have that are held higher oftentimes create a stronger dissonance
- The more dissonance, the more pressure there is to have those feelings of discomfort again.

What's amazing about this, is that cognitive dissonance is something that you see in many different areas of life, and oftentimes, this is seen especially when there is a conflict of beliefs, and oftentimes, you may not even realize it's happening until it's too late.

Let's take this example: you want to be more environmentally friendly, but then you buy a minivan that has really bad gas mileage.

Your idea is that you want to help reduce your carbon footprint, but then the conflict if you're driving a car that isn't good for the environment, perhaps because you believe that it will help you get the kids to soccer practice better, is at the forefront.

You see this as well with people who say that they are against materialism but then will get themselves a bigger house.

Usually, the dissonance is settled in one of two ways. They either sell the car to get a more environmentally friendly car, or the person practices minimalism and ends up getting a smaller place for themselves, and encourages familial minimalism.

Or you have the second option where they may minimize the dissonance that they feel when there is a responsibility to the environment. Sometimes, they may just explain it off, justifying their own reasoning, or maybe they'll use public transit or ride their bike whenever possible, or try to walk everywhere. Maybe the solution to the home is figuring out more home-efficient means in order to help reduce the environmental impact on the home.

This theory essentially shows that they will actually continue to do things, even if it's bad for them.

You see this a lot, especially in those who smoke.

Smoking is very unhealthy, and it can lead to death in many cases, but there are people who know that they can die if they continue smoking but will still do that.

Why is that? Well, they believe that they will either say that it's worth having the health drawbacks. Another way that they do it is also minimize these drawbacks. The smoker will from there, convince himself that if they continue to smoke, they won't gain weight, and if they do stop smoking, they'll end up gaining weight, and they understand that they use this to help cope with not gaining weight.

Another good one is when a smoker says "yeah, I know it's bad for me, but I also have higher anxiety, and this helps calm me down." Smokers are really good at explaining the dissonance.

Take someone who knows they're an alcoholic but refuses to change. They will either quit completely and they'll work towards it, or they'll try to explain it away by saying "if I don't drink, I'll get killer headaches, and it keeps my thoughts in check." But does it really?

No, you're not solving the problem. It's like putting one of those tiny band-aids on a large, festering wound. You might believe it's doing something, but in reality, it is harming you more than helping you.

How Does This Relate To Gaslighting?

Simply put, cognitive dissonance is another tool of narcissistic abusers. This is because it is used by narcissistic abuse, and oftentimes is a form of gaslighting in a sense.

This is where they will create confusion, unreality, and a mindset where you can't just other people.

Cognitive dissonance doesn't always happen with abuse. In fact, some people may believe that gaslighting is separate, but it is something that does happen because many times narcissist will use this as a form of a snapshot.

With gaslighting, oftentimes there are more covert means to this, and there are more barbs usually when commenting on what people do, but there is cognitive dissonance in some gaslighting.

So, let's talk about an example. You have the abuser, who meets someone they can manipulate, and they will immediately profess their love, saying that it's "fate" and they'll even get to the point where they want a marriage date in place.

The partner starts to fall for it, and they end up falling in love with this abuser, but they don't realize that the abuser has an ulterior motive. The partner has a whole wedding envisioned and they believe that this will be the way that it happens, that they'll have this dream wedding, and everything will be hunky-dory.

Except of course it's not.

Suddenly, right before the wedding or even when the partner starts to make a comment about them getting married, the abuser suddenly changes their tune, saying that they don't want to get married and they think it's crazy. Then, they start to gaslight, saying that the person is "crazy" for believing they'd ever get married, and they will start to attack the person who believes that they want to get married. The one who has the idea of marriage suddenly feels uncertain about what it is that they want to do now, and suddenly, the blame is put on the partner. Because after all, they're clearly "rushing" things getting into a relationship.

Except here's the funny part: the abuser was the one who wanted that. The partner remembers that the abuser did discuss a future, and a wedding together.

But, the abuser was stringing the person on, and they only wanted to have control and power underneath the other person, and they will have that conflict of ideas.

The abuser doesn't want to get married, but then the partner brings forth that hey, you did agree to this, and suddenly the abuser is left with the conflict. But, instead of taking responsibility for the actions he has, and maybe working out a middle ground to reduce the dissonance, he reduces the dissonance by, of course, gaslighting and refuting the partner's claims.

Gaslighting and cognitive dissonance are one in the same coin, but you could say that cognitive dissonance is how the abuser explains away the actions that he does, and explains away why he strings along with the partner.

However, cognitive dissonance isn't actually just on the abuser, but also the one who is convinced they're going to get married. This causes confusion, and unhazy reality for all of them. This renders the person confused, reeling, and they feel heartache knowing that the ideas that they had were basically slammed completely, and it does make the person feel betrayal.

But then, the person who was gaslight starts to wonder if they were in the wrong, or they were the bad guy and if they were just overthinking this. After all, why would they get married so fast, right?

This is a common tactic many who have been abused do experience, they believe that they have one idea, only to be completely squashed in the future.

Some More Examples

Let's take some more examples, shall we?

Let's look at how gaslighting does intimately connected to cognitive dissonance.

You see it in the movie from 1944 called *Gaslight* Which happened for the main character. She was believing one thing, but the abuser was saying another thing. This, in turn, will cause the target to doubt the reality that they're experiencing and the abuser as well. The abuser will continue to act like this, in order to cause doubt in their own reality, and from there, take the power and control that they can get from this.

Of course, it's at the cost of the target's well-being.

Another example is in the movie *Sleeping with the Enemy* which came out in 1991. In this movie, the abuser was a stalker, and he would be in her home straightening the bath towels every now and then. She knew that her partner was particular about cleanliness, and when she thinks she's alone, she realizes that she's not, and this is something that the person will do in order to freak out the main character. In this circumstance, this then caused the person to be verbally abused every time the person would see this, she would comment on it, and then get torn down.

But you see this everywhere. In the office, you may do something, and of course the narcissistic coworker will say that you're not, and oftentimes will practice this, in order to help create confusion in the other person, since after all, they're "clearly not doing their job" and it's only getting worse from here. The person who is on the receiving end of this is, of course, completely confused because they think they're doing the right thing, but they aren't, and in fact, it will only get worse every time they try to refute it since they will oftentimes get torn down once again.

How To Diffuse This?

How do you diffuse this again? Well, this is diffused when the one who is at the mercy of this gaslighting and narcissists abuse gets the validation and confirmation. Validation is one of the most important things for survivors of gaslighting and narcissists abuse. This is because it will help them feel like their words are valid, and what they went through actually happened.

If they don't' have validation, they become uncertain of what's going on, and the gaslighting makes them feel like their own memory is wrong. However, with validation, it can start to diffuse this.

For those who are out and survived the abuse and gaslighting, going to therapy and voicing your own personal issues, or even journaling is good.

For those that are in a situation where they haven't left yet, I recommend journaling but doing it in a way where the other person can't find out.

However, this isn't the only thing you need to do that's because narcissistic abuse will continue to haunt you if you're not careful, and you should start to master the trauma that's associated with this especially when there is unconditional, positive validation in place. This is a good way to help you overcome the trauma, and make you feel better about recovering. You can feel empowered as you get past the trauma and grief, and being able to talk about your experiences is a wonderful way of the survivor to help reduce the cognitive dissonance that's there, and from there continue with healing. Seeing someone will help you, but you must make the choice.

We'll talk a little bit more about how you can get help from the abuse in later chapters, and we'll also discuss some of the tactics that you can use to help with escaping the abuse. Cognitive dissonance is a common issue that you experience when dealing with narcissistic abuse and this chapter highlighted what it is, and why it matters to do something about this.

Chapter 7

The Purpose of Gaslighting—What Is The Endgame?

You may wonder what the endgame of gaslighting is. Here, we'll talk about the endgame of it, and why it's important to watch for this.

All About Power

At the end of the day, this is the reason why gaslighting happens. It's a deliberate and progressive means between the person who is being gaslit, and those who are doing it. This is an insidious means to manipulate the person, and oftentimes it's done in stages, constantly repeated, with the purpose to undermine the stability of the person who is going through it.

The endgame of this is power. It really isn't much else. It's done in a way that will make the other person completely question their sanity.

This has the goal of power and control. They will completely ignore the reality of the other person, for their own sick games. It's almost like a dance, and the goal is to fully control the other person, no matter what.

Many times, they may not even be done in a way that's obvious. Sometimes, it's not even deliberate, but it can be just as harmful as a purposefully, planned-out attack.

Remember, a narcissist will do this for the sole purpose of having someone that they can control and abuse. They will do everything in their power to have complete control of the other person.

What's scary about this, is that the person who is unaware of what's going on does believe that they are crazy, and oftentimes, they will feel bad after the event, simply because they let it go on for so long.

But it isn't' all your fault. In fact, sometimes you may not even realize it.

It can happen in just about any relationship, and any dynamic. Many times, we discuss this in terms of romantic relationships. You see this a lot there sure, but you see it as well in other relationship dynamics as well.

Control Until You Can't Do Anything

The goal is to complete control. They want to create uncertainty, to the point where the other person is completely at the mercy of the other person, and they can't do anything to get out of it. The other person is the one who is controlling their thoughts, actions, and pulling the strings utterly.

This can get dangerous because it does create codependency, where the other person believes that they need to be with the abuser in order to be happy. But the truth is, they are only doing this so that the other person can have utter control, and nothing more, nothing less. Power is the whole goal here.

Start Small, Then Work Bigger

The goal of a narcissistic abuser is to slowly make the other person completely question their reality. They won't' do it right away. They will play mind games with the person that they're prying upon. However, it will actually be done for the sole reason of affecting the person's ability to tolerate uncertainty and ambiguity. This is done by undercutting the victims' sense of reality and trust, and their sense of self, and from there, it further results in confusion, and perplexity for the person that you're gaslighting. It will continuously, without fail make the person feel confused and unsure of what's going on.

They will at times wonder what in the world happened with that relationship or that conversation, and oftentimes, they will question whether they got this wrong, or whether they're just going crazy.

They will very reluctantly see the gaslighted for the person that they are, and that's because they can't believe the person could ever be like that. Sometimes, the person who is being gaslit will even say "there is no way that person could do that" when talking about the other, but the reality is, they're being played and manipulated completely, to the point where it will only hurt them.

The Perfect Puppet Masters

Here's what's scary about this. These gaslighters are the perfect puppet masters, to the point where they will render others helpless. This is something that many don't even realize until it's too late.

Before we dive into how they do this, you must understand that these gaslighters, or narcissist that use this, do have many different faces, which is why you oftentimes will see the narcissist in a completely different light.

The stages that these puppet masters go through are listed below, and this is how they abuse you:

- First, they idealize you, and that's where the love bombing and other aspects come into play
- Then, they devalue you, and from there, they'll make you feel like nothing
- Then, they discard you, and they'll just completely toss you aside since you're nothing

The beginning may be almost obvious for some. If someone sees it early on, they're being gaslit by getting away, and we'll talk about how you can handle a narcissist if you suspect that they're there. But you need to be informed of the stages of power, and why they look this way.

They will oftentimes in the first stage be almost too perfect, and they are so intense and loving that the person feels like they're with the perfect partner. They will think the relationship is reciprocated.

It's not, that's for sure.

This will then make the person feel hooked, like a drug on the person, and that's how it happens. Once you're in the state where you're addicted to the narcissist, that's when the trouble occurs. It's a honeymoon phase, but that honeymoon phase is an illusion.

The next stage, which is devaluation, and it essentially is like having a fog over the relationship. Suddenly they become uncaring and cold, and the victim's suddenly feeling like they aren't doing anything right anymore. The narcissist will turn those words that used to be loving into nothing more than criticism, and everything the victim does is wrong, and they're completely devoted. The victim suddenly feels stressed, not happy, and completely confused and unhappy. They will feel like they're walking on eggshells, because everything that they do is wrong in some regard, and that the narcissist is right.

But, the narcissist isn't, and they'll purposeful make the other person feel like they're the one in the wrong, and many times, the narcissist will toss the other person if they're not getting the attention that they want. The narcissist will from here siphon all of the power and energy that the other person has, as much as they can of course, till they leave the victim completely helpless.

Then there is the discard stage. This is basically where the victim realizes that they're doomed to end with them having the narcissist completely over their own dependence. Once this happens, the narcissist believes that the person is finally under their control, but they don't care about the wishes of the victim area. At this point, the narcissist believes that the victim doesn't exist in their life.

Sometimes, this happens when the narcissist finally leaves or breaks up with them and the victims will be left completely confused. Usually, that only happens if the narcissist has no use for them.

The narcissist is indifferent to anything that the victim needs, and sometimes, the narcissist will act like the person who suffered from this doesn't even exist in their mind.

Of course, the victim is confused, filled with emotion, and will try to fix this relationship. But, the narcissist will resist every attempt to fix the relationship, will give the silent treatment in order to bully the other person, and if there is any kind of response, it's incredibly cold and not healthy for them. The victim will become inferior to the other person, and of course, the narcissist will know that they've completely drained the victim. They believe the victim isn't useful anymore, so they'll leave and move to the next supply that they can use. They'll cut off the entire relationship in many circumstances.

Of course, ay undertaking that's used to win them back on the victims' end will only feed their ego, so they may stick around for a bit.

The goal of someone who gaslights another is control, power, and sometimes dependency.

For a narcissist, sometimes it's just getting their fill, so they'll stick with the person to get the validation until the other person proves useless, and sometimes the narcissist will go so far as to outright cheat on the victim to make the victim feel like they're worthless.

Narcissist just want power, and only care about themselves, so it's not a happy ending. The goal of gaslighting is to make the victim feel like they're nothing, and the other person is everything. It's not a fun situation, and it's something most wonderful experience gaslighting will safely say is the worst part of it.

Sometimes, the victim itself will go through a cycle, and it's the following actions:

- Disbelief
- Defense
- Depression

Usually, at first, the victim will be outright confused and can't believe the narcissist is acting this way. From here, they may try to fight back, since they know that they're right. But then, after a while since the narcissist is chipping away at the other person, the victim will experience great depression, and they won't be able to make it so that they'll be able to get out of it, sometimes constantly relying on the narcissist that's gaslighting them, since that's something that they can rely on.

Of course, when the gaslighted leaves, then you run into the plight of you're not sure what's right, and what's wrong anymore.

It creates a big problem for many people, and it oftentimes can, with the right decisions, make it harder for the person to actively get out of the rut they're in, making everything harder on them.

The goal is to control, the goal is power, and that's why, gaslighting is some of the most toxic and abusive issues that can come about, and it's important to learn how to fix them.

Chapter 8

My Personal Experience With Gaslighting

I have been gaslighted for many years. In fact, it lasted almost a decade until I said it was time for me to leave, and I got away.

It was from my stepmother, who is a woman that only desired attention and validation. My dad quickly remarried after his first wife passed, and the first, the woman was very nice. She did the love bombing and acted like I and my brother were great kids. She would talk about how good we were, how she was excited to finally be a family, and actually wanted to be a parent.

I was young, and of course, I fell for that.

She did actively try to act like a good person, and she used my dad's feelings to make sure that she strung him along long enough for him to put a ring on her finger. When they got married, that's when the honeymoon phase went away, and that's when the real trouble began.

She was a narcissist, and she would make sure that her children were seen as the golden children, and my brother and I were the scapegoats. No matter what we did, it would always be wrong.

At first, it was little things. I would clean the bathroom, and she would get mad because it wasn't up to her standards. But she never came forward about those standards. I would do it again, and she would still find it wrong, and not good enough.

Every time I did something, she would always remember it differently. I would tell her that I remembered putting the permission slip for school on the kitchen table, but she will "conveniently" forget. I remember one time she said, "well maybe you should listen to where I tell you to put things and this wouldn't be lost." Except she never did.

She got a dog at one point, and she said that this would be her baby, her responsibility. However, she quickly put the responsibility on my brother and I. Her children never took care of the dog, so I was always walking, playing with it, always spending time with it. But she did claim it was her dog. I asked her if there was any way she could spend time with her, she would quickly say she couldn't, she was "too busy" and she didn't want to take care of the dog.

But of course, she bought the dog originally for herself because she wanted a dog but refused to take care of it.

The gaslighting only got worse. Every time I'd do anything, it would always be refuted. I remember one time I got grounded for a month because I weeded the garden incorrectly, even though I clearly did it right, she was just trying to make me feel like nothing.

She did this because I could see through it after a bit, but the problem was, being under the age of 18, it was hard to really craft the independence that I needed, and I was under her thumb.

I remember I used to run track, and I would screw up. She would compare me to my brother and say: "you know, maybe if you trained harder and stopped being ill-prepared, you'd actually win a race."

But I was always prepared, I was always doing the right thing.

She did hold her other children on a pedestal and forced me to call her mom even though I never saw her as a parent. She would, every time I would try to be independent, would squash it, and she would also be incredibly narcissistic towards me. She would take away belongings that aren't mine, and make sure that every time I asked her, she would immediately justify it by saying "I paid for it, so it's technically mine, and you're grounded, so I'll take your clothes away."

It did a number on my sanity, and my own personal wellness, but the saddest part of this was that I didn't know what was going on. It was like, I was put in this situation with a narcissistic parent, or whatever you'd call her, and I didn't have a way out.

I wanted to leave, because I would stand up for myself, she would just refuse it, making me feel awful.

I finally got away, but the road to recovery took years. Finally believing in myself and not doubting my every action took a lot of time, and I learned from this that people can manipulate you really badly. It isn't good. It can be terrible, and I wasn't able to be who I was for nearly a decade due to her influence.

I did eventually cut ties with her, and unfortunately, my dad stuck by her, but I didn't want to live with a narcissist in my life anymore. She did eventually toss me after using me. I always felt confused about what was right and wrong, what she wanted out of me, and when I stopped catering to her every need, she did toss me out of her life.

Familial gaslighting is hard because they are your family, but with the right understanding of what's going on, and a way to harness getting out of there you'll be happier.

I did experience this with a coworker one time as well, where it was always his way, and he would never believe anyone. He was always the one who was right, and when I left, I started doing better, was more successful. Leaving is the hardest part, but I'll tell you how to cope with this.

Chapter 9

How To Cope With Those Who Gaslight You

Coping with gaslighters isn't easy, but here, I'll go over how you can overcome the trauma of gaslighting, so you're not affected by you

Types Of Gaslighting

There are different types of gaslighting you should be wary about, and they are as follows:

· Withholding: the gaslighted doesn't listen or won't listen. The more you talk, the more they'll pretend that you're the one confusing them

· Countering: basically tells you that your memory of a situation is incorrect, so you doubt the memory

· Blocking or Diverting: literally changes the subject, will brush it off and say you're imagining things. It's proof that they're gaslighting you.

· Trivializing: they pretty much belittle your feelings so that it doesn't really matter. It'll make you feel like maybe you're overreacting, but chances are, you probably aren't.

· Forgetting or denial: This is the "I never said that!" sort of claims. This is where the person completely denies what happened, where they said they would pay for something, but then when confronted they tell you that you're the one who is supposed to pay for it, and "They never said that."

Obviously, these types are easy to see when you break it down, but what are the telltale signs your partner is indeed gaslighting you? Read below to learn.

Understanding The Signs

There are signs in place when you're being gaslighted. Here, we'll discuss what the signs of these are, and why they matter.

First, they'll say that you're the one who is imagining things. They'll say that you didn't see anything when you clearly did with your eyes, and your gut is telling you that the person is lying, but insist that you're the one in the wrong.

They will also say that you're overreacting. Every time you call them out, they say that, and while you don't think you're overreacting they will always say it. The other person may not think it's a big deal, but here's the thing, you're entitled to the feelings you have, and if you are uncomfortable with something you're allowed to speak up.

Another sign is you feel your confidence starting to dwindle a little. Remember they will try to make you question everything that's done, and if you feel like it's being belittled every time you speak to someone, then it's high time you kick them out of your life.

Also, look and see if there is an imbalance in a relationship. It's normal to have a little bit of an imbalance, but if it's so much that the other person is always fighting for the upper hand, and is controlling everything, then it's time that you do something about it. If you always feel like the other person is getting their way, it may be a sign that yes, they are, but that's because they're abusing you, not because they care.

This does make you feel like you're not good enough. You feel like you'll never measure up to what the other person wants, or what they desire. You often times will feel like they're trying to make you feel like you're not worth their attention. Sometimes they may even say that you're not pretty enough, or smart enough for another person, which can hurt a lot.

You may notice this person kind of has a Dr. Jeckyll and Mr. Hyde type of personality. Oftentimes, gaslighters will be super nice to you early on, and then, later on, start calling you crazy, and then is a total dick towards you. That's incredibly common, and oftentimes, that darker self comes out at the most random of times. You have to understand that he's not the type of person you think he is, and he's someone different from the façade.

You also may feel confused and clouded every time you're around the other person. You don't know how to talk to them and oftentimes will feel like you're in a fog just trying to get a grasp on what's going on. They are really good at making confusing conversations too, since the whole goal is to deflect blame and such on you, and they'll turn conversations about them into faults on your end.

You also should notice that you're apologizing a lot. This isn't just one or two "I'm sorry" here and there, it's actually almost all the time. They have that uncanny skill at turning arguments to make yourself feel like you're the one at fault. Of course, while you may not be faultless in everything that's going on, you need to understand that there are some things which you shouldn't be taking the blame for, and if you notice you're doing that, you can thank the gaslighted for that.

You oftentimes feel unhappy, but you feel like you can't leave. You oftentimes feel this especially when you're in an abusive relationship. The gaslighter will make you feel like you're going to be miserable without him, so that's why he convinces you to stay. But it doesn't have to be like that. You can always find someone else. If the gaslighted is a parent, understand that family isn't the end-all of bonds, and you can form your own family with friends that you find along the way, that love you.

If you notice that they're always turning the tables on the conversation, trying to make it all your fault, then that's a sign you've got a narcissistic gaslighted there. They can't do anything wrong, and they won't accept criticism ever, but every single grievance that's out there is put on you. However, you need to learn how to protect yourself against criticism, and know the weaknesses in your relationship, and work on them. Don't let them control how you feel though, because it'll only make you feel worse.

Finally, they'll say that you don't trust him. Which, you probably don't, but they will purposefully make it so that you're the one who is the bad guy, that you're the one that's causing trouble. However, you have a reason not to trust them. Plus, the gaslighted will make huge stinks about it too, to the point where it's trying to make you feel guilty. And of course, apologize to the other person as well.

Those are the signs, so what can you do about it?

7 Techniques To Disarm Narcissists So You're Not Under Their Control

There are a few things that you can do in order to disarm narcissist and not make them have control over you. Here, we'll highlight 7 of the best techniques to stop this in the tracks, and how you can take back your life.

Record It!

Some say this may be a little bit excessive, but here's the thing, it's a great way to disarm a narcissist that's gaslighting you. This is the best way to prove to the other person that they are lying, and it stops the abuse completely. You can write down what he says, or even record this with your phone, and take the note. Put the date down if you're writing it down, and if the narcissist asks, just say you're jotting down a quick note. So, when they try to turn it on you, to make it so that you're the one in the wrong, you literally have video evidence that he didn't say that.

Of course, he will try to weasel out of it, but recording is the best thing. If nothing else take those notes and try to keep everything in place.

Don't Engage

Engagement is how the person gets their upper hand. It's how they get a rise out of you. But if you know this person thrives on arguing and engagement the best thing to do is to not engage with it.

Keep the conversation with the narcissist as simple as possible. If it's a partner, then you might have some issues doing this, since they'll be around a lot. But, if you can, try to not get into it.

Remember, narcissists want to put you down, make you feel like you're doing something wrong, and if you're not groveling at their feet, they're not interested. Stop that in its place, and don't engage with that person. It's better for your own sanity and wellness if you don't engage with the other person, and sometimes it proves quite useful if you don't.

If you notice that they're trying to talk to you, especially if it's a narcissist in the office or a parent, you can use the old "oh man I didn't know what time it is, I have to go" excuse, and then skedaddle on out of there. The narcissist won't be able to do anything about it if you're quick enough.

Some may think that It's a bit of a petty technique, but the narcissist doesn't care. They want you to purposefully stumble and fall, and you'll want to get away from them as fast as possible.

Don't Take The Bait!

Narcissists will bait you. The bait is how they get you to react and how they will start gaslighting and abusing you. If you don't take the boat, they will get angry yes, but if you don't get angry back at them, so then they can squash you, then you'll be much better off.

A narcissist will get mad when you don't give them the boat, and if you act like you don't care about what they're doing. You can respond to them in a calm, collected manner in order to explain why you're not saying much or give a clam answer in response to whatever is going on. However, also understand that you don't have to tell a narcissist why you're not engaging whatsoever, and it's best if you don't talk to them for too long.

When they do bait you, understand that the narcissist wants to get a reaction out of you, and you need to not give into that. Don't give them the response that they want, and you can stay in power by giving them both logic and facts.

You also need to be careful about what you share with them. This might be hard if the person is a boyfriend or girlfriend, but you need to understand that being selective will help with this. You should make sure not to give out too many personal details, since they will use that ammo against you later on, and it's better if you just keep everything at bay, so you're not affected by this.

Set Boundaries

Boundaries are the next step. Boundaries are how you protect yourself from the narcissist, and this is something you'll have to figure out by yourself.

You should sit down and figure out what you'll take and not take from the narcissist. This is how you handle conversations with them. From there, you want to write it down, and communicate it to the narcissist that you don't want to talk about certain things with them and are fine with other things.

You should have a clean copy that you can look at very close by, so that you're not getting into the intricacies on what you will accept, and what you won't accept.

Now, let's talk about the practice of this. When you use this, you need to keep these boundaries in mind. Always understand what you're willing to and not willing to accept from them. The narcissist may follow this to the point, but sometimes, they will try and overstep.

That's when you shut them down.

You can shut them down by simply saying you're not going to listen to them. Make sure they don't interrupt and confuse you. You should always have an exit plan when dealing with a narcissist.

Always make sure that you're willing to follow through with the punishment that you put in place if the narcissist doesn't follow boundaries. You should never bluff on this, because they will be angry, and from there test the limits more. You can always leave, and you should get used to leaving someone who is doing this because it's not healthy for you.

Empathize With Feelings

You should be careful with this one, but a good way to stop a narcissist is to empathize with them. This is something you're probably already doing since you've got a lot of empathy, but oftentimes, even the most caring of people don't understand how to empathize with someone.

This is basically killing them with empathy. I suggest using this one if the narcissist is someone that you see at work and not someone you're living with. One way to stop the rage of a narcissist is to empathize with what's going on. Literally say: "You sound very hurt, and I can understand why you feel that way."

The best way to do this is to make it about the other person. Remember, narcissists love talking about themselves, and if you turn the conversation on them, they'll stop throwing insults at you, and instead talk about themselves. You see this with narcissists whenever they're family. They will immediately jump on the train of talking about themselves, maybe completely ignore you, and only focus on themselves.

Stop Apologizing to Them!

This is something you're going to need to stop doing. You need to stop apologizing so much to this person.

Granted, we're all human, we screw up, we make mistakes. Apologizing is going to backfire if you do this so much. Narcissists want you to constantly grovel and apologize to the other person. It's terrible for your self-esteem, and if you feel like making yourself wrong all the time, and not stand up for yourself, then continue to do this.

Every time you apologize to a narcissist, though it makes it work. The ego will inflate, and once you continue to do that, it's basically giving them the green light to say that they're perfect, and you're a flawed and insecure person.

And of course the target they should be going for.

Apologizing is something many people who are subjected to narcissists do. After all, when you're being blamed, you're going to continue to apologize. But, you need to stop apologizing.

How do you do that? Well, start to build up your self-esteem! This is the easiest way to do it is to understand that your self-worth and experience is more important than what some person thinks of you. You need to understand that if you have confidence, you can leave. You must understand that, and you need to realize that you're better than what they think you are.

Overly apologizing is just going to damage you more and more, and it's better if you don't do that, for the sake of your own sanity, and wellness too.

Accepting That You Can't Change Them

You need to accept that they won't change. Here's the hard truth: narcissists won't change. They will continuously act like this and will continually act like this until they find you worthless and toss you to the side.

But that doesn't mean that you should accept the treatment. You should understand that you can't change someone's personality disorder. You want to understand that so that you don't take it personally, or even as hard as you do currently.

Accepting this is one of the first steps to understanding your narcissist. They won't change. They may sometimes be nice but do understand that they'll go back to the same old, same old over a short period of time, and you don't need to subject yourself to that. You need to understand that it's not your job to change a person, but instead, you should accept that hey, they won't be changing anytime soon, so they will continue to act like that. It's much better to accept that than to just let that continue down that path.

However, just because you can't change them, doesn't mean that you can't change how you respond to them.

That means you can learn how to disarm these narcissists. You should try to kick them out of your space.

Accepting that it isn't your job to change them is one of the best things you can do to overcome the gaslighting a narcissist does. Even just responding better to them will stop this. You're not responsible for what they do, or how they react, but instead, you're responsible for your own sanity, and your brown wellness.

Never expect apologies either. They don't' know how to apologize, and oftentimes, they'll just turn it on you and blame you. Accept that they won't change, and accept that they'll start arguments over trivial matters, and from there, move on.

Ask About Things That Interest Them

Finally, a good way to disarm your narcissist is to have them talk about themselves. This works well with pretty much any type of gaslighter. Turn the topic back to them, rather than onto you, and you'll see the magical change this makes in the conversations between both of you. Narcissists do love speaking about themselves, what they're doing, and are very keen on belittling you. But, turn it on them, and they'll start talking all about themselves, and it's less of a burden on you.

This isn't the end-all to it of course, but if your narcissist is your mother for example, and you start to talk to her about her love life and what's going on, or any fun trips, you won't have to worry about her harping on you, and you won't need to worry about her getting on your case.

This is a good way to dispel narcissist, and you should always consider this tool if you're planning on dealing with them, rather than leaving.

The Final Choice: Leaving

Finally, you can leave. I highly recommend it if you can, if you're able to understand what's happening to you. The reality of gaslighting is this: the person will never change. They won't' do better, and you'll always have this person acting this way. For abusive boyfriends, do you really want to stay with a person that does that? Do you feel like it's worth it?

It's not. A narcissist will only damage you further, so you should work on a plan of leaving.

Talking to someone, see if they're willing to help you level, and making the choice to leave and not engage is the best choice for you. If it's a coworker if you can find a better job, do that. If it's a boyfriend, you need to break up with them.

If it's family, disengaging from the narcissist is your best option. However, do understand that, when you do this, you're always putting yourself at the risk of fallout from your actions. Understand that this won't be easy, but we'll talk about how you can recover from the gaslighting and narcissism that you experienced with that person.

You don't need to sit here and take it. That's what a lot need to understand. Taking the treatment will only make you worse, so never push yourself into that direction if you can. Be smart, and be logical with your choices, and understand that there is always hope, that you can always leave.

Chapter 10

How To Recover From gaslighting

How do you recover from gaslighting?

The answer to that is that it takes a very long time to recover from this. That's because gaslighting has lasting, real effects, and the abuse can last a long time. Here, we'll discuss how to recover from gaslighting in a way where you can feel liberated, and happy as well.

Understand What You're Dealing With

You need to identify what happened, and what's going on before you can do anything else. In many cases, people will not recognize it for what it is because you aren't really aware of what's going on, and you're confused. The confusion is purposeful because people will do it for the sole reason of making others feel terrible. When you do this, you won't understand as well because confusion is one of the symptoms of gaslighting. You need to understand the tactics, and you should make sure that you spend some time understanding the signs, and then go from there.

Get Out!

This is the next step, and while it's obvious, you need to do it. Understand that, until you're fully out of contact with them, if you're with the gaslighted, you'll be manipulated in some way since they know how to control you. If possible, break things off with the person if you can. If it is a family member or someone you've had an intimate relationship with, it's clearly nowhere near as easy, but it's very important to understand that the sooner you get out of there, the better.

If you can't fully break it off, you'll need to reduce your interactions and make it so that the interactions are practically nothing. But do understand that leaving any gaslighted can be dangerous, so understand that, if you think your life is in danger, call law enforcement and get support, and take the necessary.

How To Handle Yourself

When you are finally freed, or in the process of getting out, you should always be gentle with the way you handle yourself. You should make sure not to overly blame yourself for this and understand that it's hard to recognize gaslighting you should understand that self-criticism is very common, and it's a symptom of gaslighting. Letting go of this and acknowledging that this person is a total manipulator who used you is a good way to go about it. You need to accept it as a life lesson, and you should learn that, through recognizing, you gain an understanding of the experience, and get better about handling it too.

You need to start to love yourself too. Don't get upset about this, but instead, you need to learn from the experience, for the sole reason of recognizing the warning you didn't before.

When you do spend time working towards understanding yourself and getting better with gaslighting, you'll be able to get yourself properly equipped to learn from the mistakes of the past. You need to educate yourself through some books that will help you learn about gaslighting, but also learn from other sources such as podcasts, and you'll be able to, with this information, work with trying to understand and get away before things get worse.

You may start to see everyone as a gaslighted for a while. This is the "once bitten, twice shy" mentality that you're going to develop, and oftentimes, you may not realize that you're being overly cautious. But, if you've been manipulated for so long, you're going to realize that this is a pattern that happens over a period of time, and the different settings. Learning from your mistakes is one of the best things to learn, and people don't realize that, while you can screw up every now and then, you're going to realize that this will only help you if you learn about the signs, but also move on.

Moving on is going to be hard. It won't be something that you're going to do right away. You may consider isolation for a bit, but it's not ideal. You should learn to love yourself again, learn to understand yourself and get a feel for yourself over time.

Surrounding Yourself With Love

Surrounding yourself with love is a big part. You should make sure that you have people that do and appreciate you. You need to surround yourself with positivity and make sure that you are surrounded by people that will love you.

You should talk to people that you trust about your fears and doubts that have been plaguing your life. This is something that is cathartic for you because even just an acknowledgment that you're not alone can be great for you.

But along with that, when you surround yourself with people that you love, you should also get people that will validate your reality as well. They may offer some advice, or just tell you that you understand what's going on. This will make you feel great.

Sometimes, you'll feel alone, and if the person who was gaslighting you were family, it can be very hard to overcome this. But, one of the best things you can do is figure out a support group. You'll realize that you aren't alone, and you can always go out and find some other groups out there, with people who are like-minded and can help. If you go to those group meetings, you'll be able to validate the experience and talk about the trauma.

And the best part about these groups is you can talk about people who also have gone through a similar experience can benefit from you talking to the other person about the issues at hand. You'll be able to be validated which is good if you feel the impact of the self-doubts that are there.

Self-doubts will happen, but you should have a support network. You should also if you have the wherewithal to do so, try and work on yourself. Consider some new hobbies to try and learn, because it will help with overcoming the trouble you've been through. Many don't realize just how helpful it can be to work on yourself.

Plus, if you're working on yourself during this point, you can take yourself back. Remember, it's hard to deal with the trauma of the past, but that doesn't mean you have to deal with it for the rest of your life. You can learn to be yourself, be the person that you want to be, and you'll be happier than ever before. Sometimes taking control of your life again will change things, so remember that.

Exercise Caution

So many who start to be themselves after all this time struggle with being willing to trust others. It will be hard to recover from the impact of gaslighting, but here's the thing: you should exercise caution when trying to pursue new relationships, whether it be an intimate relationship or otherwise, but you should also start to be yourself. Be willing to trust your judgment and the perception that you have.

If you are happy with the person, then that's fine. It's good to be happy with your choices. But also, be smart, and also understand that if you think there is something wrong, you should consult others about it.

If you get into a relationship with someone or are trying to repair a friendship, or maybe starting a new job after leaving your prior workspace, you should always be on the lookout for anything that seems off. However, you should also not let yourself be held back by the trauma of the past. Talk to others if you have any suspicions of gaslighting, and if you notice that they're doing things that the person in the past did, such as love bombing and acting great, but then suddenly changes whenever you're closer to them, get out. You should see the red flags as soon as possible, and always be on the lookout.

Remember, you don't have to isolate yourself from relationships, but the smart thing to do is to work on trying to make sure that you understand what it is you're going through, and also, understand what it takes to learn to be trustworthy of yourself once again.

If you ever feel a bad gut feeling when you start to get into new relationships with someone, listen to it and don't think it's just your body trying to play tricks on you. Chances are, it's something that is amiss, and if you notice it, you should listen to it, and understand the truth of the matter.

Sometimes when you notice these things such as that gut feeling in your stomach, it's a sign that something is going on. But, other signs of anxiety also come up, and you should start to recognize them.

If you feel a bit of judgment when you notice it, you should acknowledge it, and actually, listen to it. That way, you'll be able to understand when that feeling comes about and become more knowledgeable of it.

Ignore The Motives

One thing to understand is that if you do wonder what the motives are, you should always make sure that you ignore it. Here's the thing, trying to understand why someone would gaslight you isn't going to help. In fact, it's going to make you feel as if you're going crazy. The problem with trying to find the answers to this is that if you continue to think about it, you're going to go crazy.

You should never try to figure it out, but instead, you should label the behavior that's there as what it is, and that's gaslighting. You should acknowledge that, and if your mind starts to wonder why it's happening, you should shut it down.

Understanding the motives of why someone would abuse you is only going to make you go crazy, and sometimes, it's better to just ignore the motives at hand, and from there, work to get out of the situation before it gets worse.

You don't' need to stay in a place that's abusing you, and you can recover. The reality of it is simple: gaslighting is terrible, is hurtful, and not good for you to deal with. If you continue to obsess love why someone does what they do, you're going to feel worse. But, instead you should be honest with why it's happening, and understand what is going on, but you should also take the time to recover and getaway.

Getting away is only the first step though. The road to recovery does take a long time. I highly recommend that, if you've been abused for a long time in this way, or have a lot of hurt and trauma from this, you should see a therapist for this. The therapist can help you work out the trauma, so you're not facing it alone.

Remember, anyone can recover from the effects of gaslighting, and you should, with the right mindset and ideas, work towards a brighter future for yourself, and for your own life. You don't need to be the effect of your past, but instead, you can learn to embrace it, and build a future that helps you, and makes you happier as well.

Chapter 11

How Gaslighting Is Used In Our Lives

Gaslighting is something that's used in different areas of life. Here, we'll discuss how gaslighting is used by other people, and how it can affect our well-being:

Gaslighting In Workspaces

Gaslighting in the workplace is much more common than you'd think. It is usually the result of manipulative and cruel bosses, who will purposefully make your life a living hell.

Sometimes it is the coworker, who is trying to one-up you and seem like the perfect person in front of the boss, but that isn't always the case.

Sometimes this shows itself whenever your coworker or boss tells you something, and later on, they'll say "oh I never said that," or "that's completely different from what I said!" Of course, the goal is to make you feel at fault, and you feel confused.

It does breed confusion, even in the workspace.

Let's take an example, shall we? So your boss wants you to run an ad campaign, and he says that he wants you to do it in two weeks. That's fine, so you put it down in your schedule. However, a week later, your boss comes storming in, threatening to terminate you without any severance pay if you don't complete it today.

But you swear it was supposed to be done the week after, right?

Now here's where it gets messier. So your boss will make you do it, and you do it, but then they can completely turn the tides *again* and then ask you why the heck you did it, and you'll start to wonder what's true, and what's not. You'll feel frustrated, and you start to wonder how come you keep forgetting all these dates.

But remember, you swore it was then, but your boss is saying something else. It'll send you in circles in confusion if you have to deal with this, which is why I always encourage you to write down everything that you must.

Here is another example. So your coworker who is a narcissist, and you hear that your boss is talking badly about you. So, you start to harbor anger towards your boss. You confront the person, and they didn't say anything. You go back to the coworker and ask why they lied, and of course, the coworker will say that they "never said such a thing."

It's insidious, but this can start to create a pattern over time. It may not seem like much now, but remember, it doesn't take just one instance, but a variety of many different experiences to create gaslighting.

Now, of course, there is the element of hey, maybe you heard something wrong. Maybe you did get the date wrong, and you can apologize. But if you notice that your boss is continuing down this trend, making you feel like garbage, and you're starting to doubt yourself, then chances are, there is something else pulling the strings here, and that something else is of course gaslighting.

You even see this in the casually racist, sexist, or bigoted bosses that some people have. You could've sworn you heard your boss make racist comments, and you did hear their derogatory words. But, when you confront the person, they say: "oh I said no such thing" and they'll get mad at you, and say you're overreacting. They will always teak the idea around in order to make it about themselves, and that will, in turn, make it so that you're getting in trouble, not them.

What's the best way to handle gaslighting in the workspace? That is, of course, to document everything. If you get harassed, document that. If you feel like you're getting dates wrong or hear something initially, always document it. You can record it as well, and also make sure that you have another coworker with you if you feel like you need that second person to solidify what's said, and to verify it.

You should try to not speak to them outside of written communication. Get it in writing. Why is that? If you get it in writing, it will bring a point of reference to it, and you'll be able to re-affirm everything, including your own self-worth and what's good. You'll be able to also, combat any sort of doubts that others will try to plant in your mind. That way, whenever they do try to gaslight you, you've got the armor that you need in order to prevent this from getting worse as well.

It's a wonderful way to ensure that you're not the one getting burned here, and you're the one who is doing the right thing. Plus, it stops the gaslighting in many cases.

Make sure that you're also getting respect too. If you notice there is something going on, record it, and report it to HR. they will take your side if you notice this, especially if you have documentation in place.

Gaslighting In Politics And Society

Politics is one of the key places where you see gaslighting. It's something that you see almost all the time these days, and Trump is probably one of the prime examples of gaslighting.

"Oh, I never said that!"

But they did. Here's an example: remember when Trump said he would protect LGBT rights, but then, later on, is found to be pushing for people in office that are anti-LGBT? And when confronted he said he never said that?

There you go, that's gaslighting. You see this a lot of times when there is a chance for someone to get in office. Trump has even said that what you see and read isn't what's happening. So, while you might think you have a grasp of what's going on, you really don't.

There are even videos that will doctor the technology in order to make a politician look good and bad.

Here's the thing: Trump isn't the only person to do this, however. Trump used this, but other politicians in the past have also used this. It's a common tactic that's used in order to gain some traction and political support.

Remember the "fake news" that Trump talks about? That's another example of gaslighting. During the 2016 election, there was Russian intervention reported, but of course, he said it was "fake news" and will still hold this as fake news to this day. But, what's hilarious is that intelligence agencies have proven that this happened.

There is also the statement he made that he had a record-breaking attendance during his inauguration, but then, when you look at the pictures, there were not too many people. These are all documented too, but every time it's prompted, it's always tossed to the side.

Usually, gaslighting is used by narcissists and sociopaths, and this is to be expected from some of the political figures. For example, trump definitely does have symptoms of a sociopath and narcissistic personality disorder. Many of the trump supporters, when they hear about this, won't question anything either, and they oftentimes are deluded into believing that it's that way.

But he isn't the only president to have used this. For example, the Clintons also used this. Look at anything that Hilary has been accused of. She will always deny it never happened.

The politicians use this with the whole intent of trying to confuse all of us. It's a psychological maneuver for everyone, the populace of America and otherwise, to be manipulated.

Another good example is, of course, the Brazilian rainforests. The rainforests there supply much of the oxygen to our planet, but they've been burning it to make room for farmland. Of course, when they do it, they completely deny that the rainforest is a big part of our health when in reality, it's part of the lungs of our planet. People will do terrible things, and from there, will deny that they ever did it, or try to justify it by saying that it's okay because people do it all the time, or that you're imagining that it's hurting the planet.

People who speak out will immediately get gaslighted. That's because politicians want to say what people want to hear, and they will then make empty promises, but then shortly after, turn it on the other person, and say that they never promised that. "Those nasty Democrats are always the ones saying that I would never do such a thing." But, there is something that it's happening, and that you're gaslighting others.

How do you overcome gaslighting on a political level though? You don't personally know these people, they just tell you what you want to hear, and what needs to be said, but then will turn on it. The answer, I want to recognize the people who are manipulating. Understand Most politicians won't actually do anything about it, and you're being duped. While you can't change the masses at times, especially if they've been duped hardcore, you can recognize it for what it is.

Understand that the "fake news" is really just gaslighting being used in politics in order to get those that support Trump, those who are pundits and intellectuals, to follow through on what he says. This may seem absurd for some people because after all, can people really be gaslighted this heavily? The answer is yes.

The reason being is because they hit at the weakness: education and vulnerabilities on a mental level.

Those who just buy off everything trump says usually just goes with it because he's a republican. Many people will just follow what he says because well, he's the representative and they've always voted red. They don't recognize when he's lying, or they refuse to.

Many of them believe that Trump will make America great again, that he will build the wall and create a more homogenous America. But has he?

One sign will tell you that he doesn't mean what he says. He's a businessman too, and oftentimes, he'll say this stuff to get into positions of power.

The scariest part about this, however, is that you really can't do much about it. After all, getting up and trying to change the masses' opinion when all of them just blindly follow what someone else says isn't going to get you anywhere. But instead you need to understand the red flags, and if you notice they're saying that what you read about and what you see isn't what's really happening, then you should take precautions.

Politicians will divert our attention from the issues that are big to other problems. For example, remember the Epstein case? Remember how that was completely diverted a week later/ That's gaslighting at the bottom of it all. There are false, misleading claims all around, and you need to become aware of it and understand that, while yes some of it is the norms of society, it's gotten so bad to the point where you need to become aware. So, that's why you should always have your wits about you and recognize it for what it is.

Gaslighting And Social Media

Social media is a cesspool for this, and it's something that most people will recognize, but oftentimes will ignore it. This is something that people will do where they'll make a big deal out of something someone said, but the other person, when confronted with that information, will say the person is "overreacting."

You hear this with issues many people will state their problems on social media, but will then say that they're overreacting, thereby denying your feelings.

People will make giant posts about how bad other people are, witch hunts oftentimes, and when they are proven wrong, they'll oftentimes backpedal and say "I never said that! You're lying."

Except, those screenshots don't' go away. You will be found out.

This is seen in many debates too. Go to any comments section on any social media site and look at the comments that are there. Some people will deny the information that's there, or bring the truth out, only to be completely rejected by others, and will be ignored. That's a form of gaslighting.

Gaslighting does happen with social media because the truth is out there, you've got to dig. Many times, if you look at the 100+ comments on an argument, oftentimes it's someone who has a really bad idea, and people are denying it, but instead of debating it, they'll oftentimes resort to gaslighting and personal attacks.

Even relationship drama can be made about fifteen times worse on social media. You'll have a couple, you think is great, but then they break up. The girl comes forward about the abuse she suffered, and what this person is really like. And there is always that person in the comments who will say that the person is lying, and deny everything, or trivialize it.

You see it a lot with the advent of the #me-too movement. A woman will come forward about how she was hurt and abused, and there are people who, instead of listening to the victim, they will ignore, or criticize those words the other has spoken.

That is a prime example of gaslighting. Gaslighting doesn't just happen in abusive relationships, it happens because someone comes forward about the truth of what they suffered from. There are times when people will completely ignore what a person is going through or try to trivialize it. But, when the proof is brought forth, people will deny it.

Social media is a hub of gaslighting. In fact, people love daytime dramas where the guy is a narcissist and the woman is coming forth about the abuse, only to be denied. Abuse is real, and abuse sometimes is brought forth on social media, and gaslighting is something most people go through, especially when trying to prove abuse.

Even just being told that you're overreacting, or denying your feelings, or telling the other person that "he's never like this" is a form of gaslighting, and once you know that, you can see just how with social media, it's a toxic tactic that even your closest friends may use.

Co-Parenting And Divorce, How Gaslighting Is Used

Co-parenting along with divorce are two of the main areas where gaslighting can be used. Why Is that? Well, oftentimes the one who is gaslighting the other will use the kids in order to get what they want.

When someone gaslights as a person who is parenting a child, it can be a struggle not just for the other parent, but also for the kids.

Some parents will paint the other parent in a bad light and will use gaslighting to make the other parent look bad.

For example, you've got a couple that is getting a divorce. They have kids. Sometimes, one parent will tell the other parent that the kid needs to be picked up from school and brought to their place by 7 pm. The parent does that, and of course, the other parent gets mad about it. Then, suddenly, the parent who was just doing what the other asked is how the bad guy.

If you're a victim of abuse from the other parent, they'll hurt you as well when the kids are involved. Sometimes, one parent who is a gaslighted will even paint the other parent as the bad guy.

I don't know if you've ever seen it, but sometimes, parents will tell their kids the other parent is going to pay for their field trip. The other parent says that's not what it's supposed to be. Perhaps both of you agreed on paying for this equally. But, the gaslighted will conveniently forget about the promise or say that it's not fair, r even trivialize it. "It's just 30 bucks, why are you making a big deal out of it?"

But it's more than just that. And what stinks is that some people will even paint the other person in a terrible light. Oftentimes, it involves a high-conflict situation for many people, since there are even custody cases where the other person gets antagonist, and the narcissist tries to get you riled up.

Many times, the narcissist in co-parenting situations will try to purposefully make it seem like you're the bad guy here. They will overstep the boundaries, maybe even give the child something you asked for them not to give to the child. For example, if the kid is not supposed to have sweets, they'll give the kid sweets because it makes them look good, and the kid is happy, and then you get mad. You tell the other person to knock it off, but they'll immediately jump into the "you're overreacting" mindset when in reality chances are you aren't. You'll be able to, with this as well, start to see how this person won't listen to your boundaries or try to overstep them. That's why, when dealing with an ex-spouse in this regard, you need to communicate with email or text, and not in person as much as you can, and try to stay detached from it as much as you possibly can.

Some co-parenting situations can turn ugly because the narcissist will try to use the child against you. For example, sometimes the narcissist will claim things, and they'll try to goad you into trying to sue the child for "fact-finding" missions. You should never use the child for information about what's happening with the other parent. If the child will talk about it, you need to do it in a way that's simple, yet effective in order to get started.

Many times, the other parent won't listen to the rules that you have in place. The purpose of that is, of course, to rile you up. The other parent will do things that will utterly annoy you, because hey, that's the goal of this. Many times, the other parent will purposefully not listen with the intent of getting you mad so you can react, and then the narcissistic parent will then tell the kid "see, your parent acts like that. They're clearly not good at their job." When in reality, you're just mad and fed up with the fact that the other person isn't even listening to your demands at all.

That's why, when it comes to co-parenting, you have to recognize what it is. If dealing with the other person just makes you feel terrible and confused, you need to understand that they will try to gaslight you. You might've recognized it when you were with them, or maybe the separation has sprung this one you.

What you need to do, is make sure that you have everything in writing, and always have the custody agreement on hand. Even if they don't listen to you, if you have it in writing, it'll help you immensely. Do that, and you'll be able to stop them in their tracks, making it easier to raise your kids, and it can help offset the blows of the attacks from the other person.

Manipulative Parents And Gaslighting

Finally, let's talk manipulative parents, and of course, gaslighting. This is the bread and butter of most of these parents since they know they can manipulate you into listening to them.

Narcissistic mothers are probably one of the worst users of this. A narcissistic mother is someone who is raising a kid as a narcissist. She will say that she doesn't think you'll amount to anything, that you're worthless, that you suck at what you do.

When you call her out on it, guess what she will do? Completely ignore it, trivialize it, or put the blame on you.

You see this especially with manipulative mothers, who want to be the one in charge. The narcissistic mother who gaslights will use you as the scapegoat. The scapegoat means that you'll be blamed for everything and anything that happens.

Every time you try to talk about it, the manipulative parent will immediately shut you down, by saying you're imagining things, that you're wrong, ignore the issue completely, or trivialize everything to hell and back.

Every time you try to engage with them you just come out feeling more confused and unsure of yourself than before. It's a struggle, that's for sure.

Many times, these manipulative parents only care about themselves. They don't' care about raising you. In fact, they might have a second kid, who they'll dub the "golden child" that can do no wrong. Every time you engage with them, they'll be quick to turn everything against you and tell you that you suck, and the golden child is better and that you don't have any worth.

Fun, isn't it?

Many times, these narcissistic and manipulative parents will try to find ways to put you down, and they will do so without any regard for how you feel. There are even narcissistic mothers who will take things from their children, and when prompted to ask what they did with it, or even why, the narcissistic mother will be very quick to trivialize it.

It's not an easy situation, that's for sure, and many times, the narcissist does stick around.

What's the solution then? How do you handle a parent who gaslights you like that?

The answer is to leave or to limit communication with them. If you've experienced this as a kid, chances are the manipulative parent has everyone around their finger. The spouse, the rest of the family, even your own siblings could be victims of this person's abuse. The answer to everything is to just figure out a way to handle the narcissistic parent, whether it be setting those boundaries, or just up and leaving.

The latter is especially hard if you're either financially dependent on them, or if you're not a legal adult, but if you notice that you're being gaslighted by the manipulative parent, the solution to that, is to figure out how to leave, and to do so right away.

You owe it to yourself to leave, and you don't have to stay. Manipulative parents aren't good for anyone, and they will oftentimes drive you to the brink before you can do anything about it.

They'll be quick to blame you, but oftentimes when you tell them that you did something, whether it be the chores or whatever, or maybe you noticed that they're lying, they'll trivialize it as much as they can.

It stinks, but that's really just the way it is with them.

The worst part of this, however, is that they won't change. You could hope, they could claim they're going to therapy to change, but it's not the case. The manipulative parent will never fully get out of the narcissistic personality, even if you ask nicely.

Gaslighting is so prevalent in our world today that it's not even funny and here, you learned about some of the forms of it, and why it's important to understand. Remember that your own sanity, wellness, and happiness involves curbing the gaslighting that happens, and you have to, with this as well, understand that it will only go away if you choose to disengage with them, and not get riled up.

Gaslighting is an epidemic, but by recognizing when it happens, and understanding, you'll be happier than ever.

Conclusion

Gaslighting is hard to deal with it's a form of abuse, and something narcissists love to use as their main ammo against you.

But remember that you're not alone. You don't have to deal with the manipulation and covert tactics to make you feel terrible.

Instead, you can recognize it for what it is, and handle it accordingly. Knowing is half the battle, and when it comes to gaslight, it's even more important than you'd think.

Gaslighting hurts you. I've been gaslighted for a year from my old parent, and when I finally left, I realized that I was being manipulated by her. She was also a narcissist, which isn't a requirement to gaslight, but narcissists love to use it.

However, you need to understand that there are different types of gaslighting out there, and so much that can happen to you. If you're not careful, you fall into the trap of being affected by it.

That's why, the next step is, if you know you're being abused in this fashion, do something about it. Don't wait, and don't sit on it any longer. I know abuse isn't easy to come to terms with, but, if you understand what it is that you're going through, you'll be happier than ever before. Do this, and you'll be able to say to yourself that yes, you've overcome the pain and suffering from the past, and you can now embrace the future!